Participating on Equal Terms?
The Gender Dimensions of Direct Participation in Organisational Change

The European Foundation for the Improvement of Living and Working Conditions is an autonomous body of the European Union, created to assist the formulation of future policy on social and work-related matters. Further information can be found at the Foundation Web site at http://www.eurofound.ie/

Participating on Equal Terms? The Gender Dimensions of Direct Participation in Organisational Change

Findings from the EPOC Survey

Annette Schnabel
Juliet Webster

EUROPEAN FOUNDATION
for the Improvement of Living and Working Conditions

Cataloguing data can be found at the end of this publication

Luxembourg: Office for Official Publications of the European Communities, 1999

ISBN 92-828-7146-0

© European Foundation for the Improvement of Living and Working Conditions, 1999

For rights of translation or reproduction, applications should be made to the Director, European Foundation for the Improvement of Living and Working Conditions, Wyattville Road, Loughlinstown, Co. Dublin, Ireland.

Printed in Ireland

The paper used in this publication is chlorine free and comes from managed forests in Northern Europe. For every tree felled, at least one new tree is planted.

Foreword

In recent years there has been a growing interest in new ways of organising work to make European enterprises more competitive in global markets. As part of this new interest in organisational efficiency, direct participation arrangements such as total quality management, quality circles, team work and re-engineering have gained in popularity. The indications are that this new direct approach to employee involvement is of benefit not only to the organisation, but also to the workforce. For the enterprise, there is the more efficient use of human resources and greater flexibility in its operations; for workers, the possibility of more meaningful jobs and a greater input into workplace issues which directly affect their working lives. In showing a greater interest in direct participation, unions and employers in Europe are seeking to develop a social model which is unique to Europe and in contrast to the emergence of workplace models in other trading blocks.

In order to address these developments, the European Foundation for the Improvement of Living and Working Conditions initiated the EPOC Project (**E**mployee direct **P**articipation in **O**rganisational **C**hange). The objective of this project was to research the trend towards more direct participation in European enterprises, and to provide information which would feed into the debate between the social partners and the European Union institutions on the most appropriate form of work organisation for Europe.

So far, the Foundation has produced nine publications as part of this ongoing research project. The first report presented the conceptual framework of the EPOC project. The second publication was based on an analysis of research which looked at the attitudes and understanding of the social partners in EU Member States, and the extent to which the application of direct participation can influence the humanisation of work while at the same time increasing profitability.

The third report reviewed empirical research into direct participation in Europe, the United States and Japan and gives an overview of the existing knowledge on the topic. It examines the extent of the Japanese 'Toyota' model and contrasts it with the Scandinavian 'Volvo' model of work organisation; and it has the most extensive literature review on this subject yet published in Europe.

Having carried out these research projects the Foundation paused to take stock, and a summary of the results so far was published in a booklet in 1996 which drew together all the knowledge EPOC had contributed to the debate. However, many questions were still unanswered and knowledge gaps remained. To fill these gaps the Foundation carried out a survey of managers in ten Member States to ascertain the extent and nature of direct participation within their establishments. The responses to this survey provided a wealth of information and the first analysis of the survey results was published in 1997.

This first EPOC report on the survey results was a significant contribution to the policy debate around the European Commission's Green Paper *Partnership for a New Organisation of Work*. It provided, for the first time, detailed information on the extent of direct participation in its various forms; its economic and social impact; the attitudes of European management to it as a process for the efficient organisation of work, and the results of involving workers and their representatives in the process of change.

As a further step in the Foundation's contribution to the ongoing debate a series of additional analyses of the results of the survey were undertaken in 1998 under the headings of: the relationship between employment, organisational flexibility and innovation; direct participation in the social public services (reports on both of these have been published); the nature and extent of group work in Europe; and, in this report, the gender aspects of direct participation, such as access, training and employment.

One of the features of the European workplace which is growing in importance is the relative position of men and women within the labour market. The gender division of labour often tends to be overlooked in discussions on changes in the organisation of work. The findings of the EPOC survey, however, reveal that there are important equal opportunities issues to be addressed by the introduction of innovative workplace arrangements. For example, they confirm the horizontal and vertical occupational and sectoral segregation of the sexes, and show that the introduction of direct participation takes place in this context. The survey also points to a stereotyping of training topics, with men having access to training in technical skills, such as data collection, while the training offered to women is in 'soft' skills, such as interpersonal relations.

Clive Purkiss   Eric Verborgh
Director   Deputy Director

Contents

		Page
Foreword		v
Chapter 1	**Introducing a gender perspective**	1
Chapter 2	**Methodology: static and dynamic dimensions of gender**	13
Chapter 3	**Gender dimensions of the survey workplaces**	31
Chapter 4	**Direct participation and gender**	63
Chapter 5	**Training and qualifications**	99
Chapter 6	**Effects of direct participation on equal opportunities**	113
Chapter 7	**Summary, conclusions and future directions**	121
Appendix		133

Chapter 1   Introducing a Gender Perspective

> The new developments in relation to work organisation present a challenge and an opportunity with regard to equal opportunities for men and women ... The question is whether the new organisation of work, emphasising social skills, broader skills and multitasks, can contribute to the promotion of equal opportunities.
>
> European Commission Green Paper, *Partnership for a New Organisation of Work*.

This report presents the results of an analysis of the EPOC survey from a gender perspective. Specifically, it considers the gender dimension of direct participation – both the involvement of women and men in direct participation practices in workplaces, and the implications of direct participation practices for equal opportunities between women and men. We are particularly interested in whether direct participation is associated with changes in the sexual division of labour and in the conditions of women's work. The EPOC survey was commissioned by the European Foundation for the Improvement of Living and Working Conditions in Dublin, and full details of the survey are contained in a report produced by the Foundation (1997). Though the survey was not designed from the outset to investigate gender issues in direct participation, it did include questions on the proportion of women in the largest occupational group, and their involvement in employee participation. From these we are able to derive a considerable amount of information on the gender differences in employee involvement in, and the equal opportunities potential offered by, direct participation practices.

The need for a gender perspective on organisational change

There are several compelling reasons for examining the gender and equal opportunities issues raised by organisational changes currently taking place in European workplaces. First, **women's employment generally is steadily increasing** in all countries of the European Union and it is assuming an increasing significance as a proportion of total employment. Over two-thirds of new jobs created in the EU between 1994 and 1996 have been filled by women, who now account for over 40% of the labour force of the European Union as a whole. In some countries, particularly the Nordic countries, nearly 80% of women are members of the labour force. Moreover, although all Member States have experienced a disproportionate growth in the numbers of women in the workforce, its feminisation has been a particularly strong feature of those economies with previously low rates of female participation – in southern Europe, for example. Women are therefore numerically very significant members of the workforce, and this significance looks likely to continue to grow as male unemployment increases and the continued expansion of services boosts labour market demand for female employees (European Commission, 1997a).

Second, **women and men continue to be segregated in different parts of the labour market**, with crucial implications for the work which they do, and for the pay and conditions which they enjoy. Sex segregation operates by industry and by occupation; on both counts, women are more likely than men to be employed in areas characterised by poor access to skills and training, by relatively low collective bargaining coverage and therefore by comparatively weak pay and conditions (European Commission 1994a). Despite over two decades of concerted policy effort, we have not yet achieved equal opportunities between women and men in European workplaces, and indeed there is now some evidence of a retrenchment of gender inequalities in employment and indeed in society as a whole (Duncan, 1996; Webster, 1996). The equal opportunities policy agenda therefore has a considerable way to go before it can be said to have been fulfilled.

Third, **recent patterns of organisational change seem to offer greater potential than ever before for improving equal opportunities in the workplace.** Contemporary organisational transformations are generally thought of in relation to their contribution to improved competitiveness, but they may also have positive implications for equal opportunities. For example, teamworking involving mixed-sex work teams may help to break down the sexual segregation of labour which assigns women and men to particular gender-typed areas of production or of workplaces. Some evidence for this development has been noted in the Scandinavian automotive industry (Gunnarsson, 1994), although there is also evidence of gender roles persisting in teamwork (Shapiro and Austin, 1996). Similarly, the dismantling of managerial layers and the consequent flattening of organisational hierarchies may be beneficial for equal opportunities: women have often found it difficult to progress in conventional hierarchical organisations where a mixture of organisational procedures and organisational culture combine to restrict their occupational possibilities; make it difficult for individuals with domestic responsibilities to progress on an equal basis with those who have none; install 'glass ceilings' with invisible barriers to promotion, and even favour networks of 'lads' (Tierney, 1995; Acker, 1992).

Emphasis on multiskilling and the need for both life skills and technical skills may also benefit women. It is often supposed that women possess life skills – and particularly social and communicative skills – in abundance. Certainly it would seem that their 'apprenticeship in womanhood' includes the development of interpersonal skills, though this is by no means an inherent quality of women, nor is it clear whether the possession of social skills will indeed promote equal opportunities in work settings where these skills are required. What little evidence there is on this point suggests that these skills are not rewarded when they are used by women because they are considered to be normal and their use is taken for granted (Woodfield, 1994).

The problems of numerical flexibility, and particularly of 'atypical' forms of employment contract such as part-time work, are widely discussed and well understood in relation to equal opportunities, in particular for their implications for the training and career progression of employees. However, potentially positive aspects of working time changes are much less well considered. It is worth noting that women's employment has never followed the same full-time lifetime pattern of men's employment; their working lives have always been much more interrupted than men's as they take time out to care for children and families and return to the labour market afterwards. Women are much more likely than men to work part-time, or in some other 'atypical' employment arrangement, which for them is not atypical at all. In this context, creative approaches to working time reorganisation, such as annualised working hours or flexible shift systems, may be very beneficial for women seeking to balance home and work. They may help to eliminate the discrimination inherent in part-time employment which has effectively denied women access to training; to the informal organisational networks which allow people to be noticed and progress within organisations, and to the personal development possibilities which follow from these. These, therefore, are some of the potential beneficial implications of organisational change which need to be considered.

Fourth, **policy has not yet fully explored the equal opportunities possibilities offered by the dynamics of organisational changes.** Indeed, in the policy domain as well as in the scientific literature, the potential of organisational change to address equal opportunities objectives is rarely articulated. Issues of organisational change and the promotion of equal opportunities are generally addressed quite separately, and it is one of the aims of this report to consider these issues in relation to one another.

To date, equal opportunities policy in the European Union has been pursued through a series of action programmes, which set the framework for policy priorities over five-year periods. Under the Third Action Programme, which ran from 1991 to 1995, the improvement of women's position in the workforce was one of the three key strands of policy, and it concentrated principally upon the provision of vocational training and support for initiatives to help women in businesses and small enterprises. The Fourth Action Programme, which runs from 1996-2000, also has as a global objective the promotion of equal opportunities within a changing economy, and in terms of work, its key focus is on desegregating the labour market, improving access to training, and encouraging women's entrepreneurship. The contribution which organisational change itself might make to the equal opportunities agenda is not explicitly articulated, although the programme's underlying policy principle is that of 'mainstreaming', which does at least imply attention to equal opportunities issues in all other spheres of policy making (including policy making for organisational change). In this sense, the mainstreaming approach should promote a greater integration of equal opportunities policies within programmes of organisational change, but this approach will of course have to be taken up in practice, on the ground.

The principle of 'mainstreaming' represents the latest in a series of approaches to equal opportunities policy making. The pressing need for achieving equal opportunities in all spheres of social and economic life has been recognised by European policy since the Treaty of Rome in 1957. Early approaches to equal opportunities were based on the principle of 'equal treatment', and enshrined in law the principle that men and women should be treated equally. However, it became clear that equal treatment did not necessarily lead to equal outcomes (Rees, 1995), and indeed the net effect of some policy programmes was to widen the gap between women and men. 'Positive action' approaches recognised that there are differences between women and men, in initial labour market position, in educational and training backgrounds, and in organisational experiences, and they aimed to redress these inequalities and compensate for disadvantage. Their principal drawback was in their failure to confront the problems inherent in ghettoised structures, whether male or female-dominated, and in their failure to attempt to develop alternative structures or cultures of work. Most recently, equal opportunities policies have taken a 'mainstreaming' approach. Mainstreaming rests on an acknowledgement that gender is one of the organising principles of society and all its structures, and that no institution or policy is therefore gender neutral. On this basis, mainstreaming centres on incorporating a gender dimension into all analysis, policy development, implementation and evaluation. It would therefore seem to offer excellent potential for incorporating equal opportunities concerns into programmes for organisational change, both at policy-making level and at a practical level, within firms themselves.

Policy thinking on organisational change, however, still has some way to go in adopting an equal opportunities programme. Organisational change is often portrayed as being gender neutral, and the differential implications for women and men are not generally discussed. Moreover, the potential equal opportunities benefits are seldom considered; organisational change is more often portrayed in terms of its beneficial effects upon economic performance and competitive advantage. For example, the European Commission's White Paper on *Growth, Competitiveness and Employment* (1994b) outlined the development of measures necessary to improve the innovative and competitive qualities of Europe's organisations, and identified a series of challenges facing them which ranged from the development and implementation of new technologies, to the adaptation of education and training systems, to improved exploitation of environmental resources. Although the paper recognised the need for a strengthening of equal opportunities for women and men in employment, it did not link this requirement to the organisational changes which it promotes. The Commission's Green Paper on *Innovation*, published the following year (1995), took up a number of these themes particularly in relation to technological innovation, identifying a series of preconditions in the spheres of research and development, human resource development, financial support and regulatory regimes, which, it argued, were necessary to overcome a fragmentary and often inhibitive environment for innovation. It did not, however, devote much attention to questions of organisational innovation or to their potential for achieving social as well as economic objectives, such as equal opportunities.

In early 1997, a further Green Paper, entitled *Partnership for a New Organisation of Work* (European Commission, 1997b), considered the dynamics currently under way within European organisations, and argued that these are undergoing a transition from 'Fordist' working arrangements to 'post-Fordist' ones – i.e. a transition from mass production of goods and services for mass markets to flexible production of customised products according to customer requirements. In this Green Paper, it was argued that the industrial system of mass production, which had dominated European industry for well over one hundred years, was becoming decreasingly well suited to the circumstances of late twentieth century European economies. Hierarchical organisations, with highly specialised and simplified functions, did not provide enough potential for innovation and creativity in European firms, and new ways of improving productivity and working conditions were sorely needed. This need became more pressing with the increasing importance of knowledge-based work to the competitive advantage of European economies, with the growing sophistication of customer markets, and with an increasingly rapid rate of technological innovation. These new developments in work organisation were seen as offering important opportunities for addressing the key challenges facing European employers and employees, and two questions were raised in connection with the gender dimension of organisational change: first, what more could be done to ensure a better gender balance through the development of a new organisation of work, and second, how far women's growing participation in the labour market might be expected to have an impact on work organisation. However, the Green Paper suggests that the salience of new organisational forms for equal opportunities lies in their widespread diffusion in the services sector, where women are strongly represented. Although this undoubtedly makes organisational change a very important issue for female employees, their numerical strength in service organisations does not translate directly into improved potential for equal opportunities. A more important question is what types of services jobs women are employed in: the growth in women's part-time employment in services makes very clear the fact that the nature of work and the conditions of work are more important in shaping women's working lives than the simple fact of work alone. Nevertheless, both of the questions raised in the Green Paper are central concerns of this report, which aims to provide some substantial empirical evidence on the relationship between work reorganisation and equal opportunities. But organisational change can only improve equal opportunities if women participate in it in large numbers. This report therefore goes further than the Green Paper, and addresses the twin issues, first, of men's and women's access to direct participation in organisational change, and second, the influence of new forms of work organisation on equal opportunities at work.

The Employment Summit held in Luxembourg in November 1997 also addressed the equal opportunities issues in employment and unemployment. The Summit recognised that, among other things, there is a persistent imbalance between women and men in certain economic sectors and occupations, and it adopted a series of guidelines for action by Member States. These guidelines included the strengthening of equal opportunities and the improvement of the adaptability of labour. Importantly, the guidelines incorporate a recognition that women's labour market position is intimately connected to their role in the domestic sphere, and therefore that if equal opportunities are to be achieved, then part of the strategy for doing so must include support for women in the meeting of their domestic responsibilities. However, again there is no explicit connection made between strategies for improving equal opportunities and the dynamics of organisational change taking place in Europe's workplaces which might have an important role to play in the equal opportunities agenda. Instead, the guidelines invite Member States to ensure that there is adequate provision of good quality care for children and other dependants. Unfortunately, no targets are set for improvements in women's employment, training and pay, despite calls from the European Parliament for this to be done.

In the light of the mainstreaming approach which is being taken increasingly seriously by institutions of the European Union and by its Member States as essential for both social justice and economic competitiveness, an analysis of the equal opportunities issues arising from organisational changes in Europe's workplaces is all the more pressing, as is the development of policy actions which are informed by a recognition of the differences between men's and women's experiences of organisational change. This report contributes to this analysis in addressing developments in work organisation from an equal opportunities – or more accurately, a gender – perspective. It considers whether women and men in the labour force enjoy equal access to direct participation

(DP) over organisational change, and it examines the evidence for gender implications, and most importantly, gender inequalities, arising from recent organisational change initiatives.

The major issues addressed in this report

This report is concerned with the different situations of women and men in relation to direct participation in the survey organisations. We therefore explicitly link direct participation to the gender composition of the EPOC workplaces, explore the properties of direct participation in different gender settings, and provide some empirical evidence for the effects of direct participation. We focus specifically on the access of men and women to direct participation (as opposed to indirect participation, which is the subject of other surveys by the Foundation and others), and the effects of direct participation on equal opportunities in access to jobs, training and qualifications. Analysis of the gender differentials of direct participation requires a concept and mechanism for identifying the sexual division of labour in the individual workplaces. The concept of 'gender structure' has been applied to the survey data for this purpose; it allows us to distinguish between different workplaces on the basis of the level of women's employment within them. Its workings and application are elaborated in the next two chapters.

The context within which direct participation takes place is the focus of the first part of the analysis in this report, and this gives rise to a series of questions which we answer in order to set the scene for subsequent discussion of direct participation.

- What industry sectors are represented in this survey and to what extent do they employ women and men?
- What are the occupational groups covered by the survey and who is employed within them?
- What patterns of employment contract are emerging and how are they distributed between women and men?
- What are the task characteristics of the work of women and men in the survey?
- What general features of employee representation can we discern in relation to the employment of women and men in the survey?

Having examined the context within which women and men are employed in the survey organisations, we can then pose a series of questions relating specifically to the gender dimension of the direct participation to which they have access. These can be summarised as outlined below.

- To what extent is direct participation practised in organisations with different gender structures?
- To what extent is the sectoral segregation of men and women affected by direct participation?
- To what extent is the occupational segregation of men and women affected by direct participation?
- Which particular forms of direct participation are particularly characteristic of women's and men's work?

Previous research into the nature of organisations in which women work, as well as our analysis of the features of direct participation, shows that gender divisions of labour, and hence processes of potential gender disadvantage, do not operate identically in every setting. Structural characteristics of firms, sectors and occupations shape the position of female employees relative to men, and indeed to each other, and thus affect the extent and form of gender inequality. Because of these differences, equal treatment for men and women (for example, in relation to access to direct participation) does not necessarily lead to equal outcomes, as equal opportunities policy makers realise. We therefore emphasise structural features of establishments which lead to differences between women as well as between the two sexes, in order to remind policy makers of the importance of differentiating in equal opportunities policy.

The organisation of this report

The next chapter of this report describes the methodology used in analysing the gender issues surrounding direct employee participation in the survey organisations. In particular, it describes the organising principles around which the data has been tabulated and analysed, and the way in which a gender dimension has been introduced into the data. Chapter 3 considers the organisational context within which gender differences in direct participation may later be analysed, and discusses the survey variables which allow us to identify the contextual features of the organisations surveyed. Chapter 4 analyses the gender dimensions of direct participation. Chapter 5 examines the training and qualification patterns of direct participation, and Chapter 6 reports management's views on the effects of direct participation by women and men. Chapter 7 offers our conclusions and identifies the issues which would benefit from further analysis.

References

Acker, J., 'Gendering organizational theory' in A. J. Mills and P. Tancred (eds), *Gendering Organizational Analysis*, London, Sage, 1992.

Duncan, S., 'Obstacles to a successful equal opportunities policy in the European Union', *European Journal of Women's Studies,* 3, 4, 1996, pp. 399-422.

European Commission, *Bulletin on Women and Employment in the EU*, Luxembourg, Office for Official Publications of the European Communities, October 1994a.

European Commission, White Paper, *Growth, Competitiveness and Employment*, Luxembourg, Office for Official Publications of the European Communities, 1994b.

European Commission, Green Paper, *Innovation*, Luxembourg, Office for Official Publications of the European Communities, 1995.

European Commission, *Equal Opportunities for Women and Men in the European Union 1996,* Luxembourg, Office for Official Publications of the European Communities, 1997a.

European Commission, Green Paper, *Partnership for a New Organisation of Work*, Luxembourg, Office for Official Publications of the European Communities, 1997b.

European Foundation for the Improvement of Living and Working Conditions, *New forms of work organisation. Can Europe realise its potential? Results of a survey of direct employee participation in Europe*, Luxembourg, Office for Official Publications of the European Communities, 1997.

Gunnarsson, E., 'Women and men – different rationalities?' in E. Gunnarsson and L. Trojer (eds), *Feminist Voices on Gender, Technology and Ethics*, Luleå, University of Technology Centre for Women's Studies, 1994.

Rees, T., *The Position of Women in the EC Training Programmes: Tinkering, Tailoring, Transforming*, Bristol, University of Bristol Policy Press, 1995.

Shapiro, G. and S. Austin, *Equality Driven Total Quality*, University of Brighton Business School, Occasional Paper No 3, 1996.

Tierney, M., 'Negotiating a software career: informal work practices and "the lads" in a software installation', in K. Grint and R. Gill (eds), *The Gender-Technology Relation*, London, Taylor and Francis, 1995.

Webster, J., *Shaping Women's Work: Gender, Employment and Information Technology,* London, Longman, 1996.

Woodfield, R., *An ethnographic exploration of some factors which mediate the relationship between gender and skill in a software R&D unit,* University of Sussex D.Phil thesis, 1994.

Chapter 2

Methodology: Static and Dynamic Dimensions of Gender

In 1992 the European Foundation for the Improvement of Living and Working Conditions launched a major investigation into the nature and extent of direct participation and its role in organisational change, called the EPOC Project (**E**mployee direct **P**articipation in **O**rganisational **C**hange).

The first phase of the project included the development of a conceptual framework of direct participation to make it more accessible to empirical research (Geary and Sisson, 1994); a study of the understanding, attitudes and approaches of the social partners in the European member states (Regalia, 1995); an appraisal of the available research in the USA and Japan as well as at national level within the European Union (Fröhlich and Pekruhl, 1996). Also, as part of the project, a number of conferences and round tables of the social partners, governments and European Commission representatives were held.

The activity in the second phase has been the design, implementation and analysis of a representative postal survey of workplaces in ten EU countries, with the objective of helping to fill the information gap which was identified by the research in the first phase.

The EPOC survey

The EPOC survey, which was commissioned by the European Foundation for the Improvement of Living and Working Conditions, was primarily intended to investigate the nature and extent of direct employee participation (direct participation, to use the shorthand). A standard questionnaire, translated with the help of industrial relations 'experts', was mailed to a representative sample of workplaces in ten EU member countries: Denmark, France, Germany, Ireland, Italy, the Netherlands, Portugal, Spain, Sweden and the UK. Altogether, some 5,800 managers, from manufacturing and services, and from the public and the private sectors, responded. The size threshold was 20 or 50 employees depending on country. The respondent was either the general manager or the person he or she felt was the most appropriate. The main subject of the questions was the largest occupational group.

In keeping with the conceptual framework developed in its early days (for further details, see Geary and Sisson, 1994), the focus of the EPOC survey was on the two main forms of direct participation, which for the purposes of empirical enquiry can be defined as follows:

- *consultative participation* – management encourages employees to make their views known on work-related matters, but retains the right to take action or not; and
- *delegative participation* – management gives employees increased discretion and responsibility to organise and do their jobs without reference back.

The essence of direct participation can be better understood by contrasting it with other major forms of involvement and participation.

Figure 2.1 *Types of involvement and participation*

information disclosure;

financial participation:
- *profit sharing,*
- *share ownership;*

direct participation:
- *consultative,*
- *delegative;*

indirect or representative participation:
- *joint consultation,*
- *co-determination,*
- *collective bargaining,*
- *board level representation, such as worker directors.*

In contrast with communications and financial participation, i.e. profit sharing and share ownership, the key distinguishing features of direct participation are consultation and delegation. Profit sharing and share ownership may be integral features of a participative approach, but they do not necessarily involve consultation or delegation. In contrast with indirect or representative participation, the word *direct* is key; whereas indirect participation takes place through the intermediary of employee representative bodies, such as works councils or trade unions, direct participation involves employees themselves immediately in the decision-making process.

Both consultative and delegative participation can involve individual employees or groups of employees. The two forms of consultative participation can be further subdivided. Individual consultation can be 'face-to-face' or 'arms-length'; group consultation can involve temporary or permanent groups. This gives us six main forms of direct participation regardless of the particular label applied. The six forms are set out in Figure 2.2, together with examples of relevant practices from EPOC's research review (Fröhlich and Pekruhl, 1996) and round-table discussions. It is around these types that the EPOC survey's questions were structured.

Figure 2.2 *The main forms of direct participation*

- **Individual consultation:**
  'face-to-face': arrangements involving discussion between individual employee and immediate manager, such as regular performance reviews, regular training and development reviews and '360 degree' appraisal;
  'arms-length': arrangements which allow individual employees to express their views through a 'third party', such as a 'speak-up' scheme with 'counsellor' or 'ombudsman', or through attitude surveys and suggestion schemes.

- **Group consultation:**
  'temporary groups': groups of employees who come together for a specific purpose and for a limited period of time, e.g. 'project groups' or 'task forces';
  'permanent groups': groups of employees that discuss various work-related topics on an ongoing basis, such as quality circles.

- **Individual delegation:**
  individual employees are granted extended rights and responsibilities to carry out their work without constant reference back to managers – sometimes known as 'job enrichment'.

- **Group delegation:**
  rights and responsibilities are granted to groups of employees to carry out their common tasks without constant reference back to managers – most often known as 'group work'.

The questionnaire did not just ask about direct employee participation, however. Mindful of the wider debates touched on in the previous section, there was also a range of questions about the other initiatives which management had been taking, including those associated with direct participation and equal opportunities. Also included were questions about the relevant context of the workplace and changes in the levels of employment over the past three years. A copy of the questionnaire is contained in the general survey report (*New Forms of Work Organisation*) published by the Foundation in 1997.

Methodology of the EPOC survey

Respondents

The EPOC survey was planned to be representative of workplaces in as many countries as the budget would reasonably allow, taking into account a range of different populations and geographical positions. The ten countries finally chosen were: Denmark, France, Germany, Ireland, Italy, the Netherlands, Portugal, Spain, Sweden and the UK. The choice of the workplace as the level and the general manager as the immediate target is explained by the overall aim of the survey, which was to gather as much data as possible about what was happening in practice. A survey directed at higher levels in the organisation was unlikely to have produced such information and there was some concern that small workplaces in particular might not have a personnel manager. In any event, the general manager was invited to complete the questionnaire him/herself or to pass it on to the manager most capable of doing so.

In targeting managers only, and not employees or their representatives as well, the EPOC survey is open to the criticism that its results are one-sided. Much as the EPOC Research Group would like to have included employee representatives, especially, in the survey, the costs of doing so proved to be prohibitive. In many workplaces it would have been necessary to get a response from more than one employee representative and in some countries there would have been enormous complexity in identifying the most appropriate respondent(s).

The omission of employee respondents is perhaps not as much of a weakness as it might at first appear, however. The main objective of the EPOC survey was to establish the nature and extent of direct participation. The experience of the Foundation's survey on *Workplace Involvement in Technological Innovation in the European Community* (Fröhlich, Gill and Krieger, 1993), which involved responses from almost 4,000 employees as well as from an identical number of managers, showed a high consensus about factual issues between the two groups of workplace respondents. Also, a unique feature of the EPOC survey was that it did not simply ask about the incidence of direct participation, which managers might have been tempted to exaggerate. Questions designed to estimate the coverage, scope and intensity of the processes involved helped to ensure a balanced picture.

Organisation of the survey

The questionnaire, which is reproduced in full in the general report (EFILWC[1], 1997), was initially drawn up in English by members of the research group, with the help of a team from the Industrial Relations Research Unit at the University of Warwick, and was translated by them and by trusted experts into the other languages. Tenders to administer it were invited in the Official Journal of the European Union in September 1995. In December 1995, INTOMART, representing GfK Europe, and based in Hilversum (the Netherlands), was commissioned to undertake the fieldwork. With INTOMART's help, the questionnaire was pre-tested in the ten countries in the spring of 1996.

Details of the main survey

The gross sample of workplaces, drawn up by the national GfK members, differed for the ten countries according to population size, the number of employees in industry and services, and the number of workplaces with 20 or more employees (for the smaller and medium-sized countries) and 50 or more employees (for the larger ones). For the larger countries (France, Germany, Italy, Spain, the UK) the gross sample was 5,000 workplaces; for the medium countries (Denmark, the Netherlands and Sweden) 2,500 and for the smaller countries (Ireland and Portugal) 1,000.

The mailing was carried out in two full waves, including the questionnaire and the accompanying letter, followed by one additional reminder letter. The first questionnaires were mailed in the beginning of June 1996. Because of the varying times of summer holidays, an additional selected mailing was carried out in certain countries with a lower response rate in October 1996, focusing on particular sectors. The additional mailing used the original representative sample.

Each of the national GfK member institutions drew up the final gross samples for their respective countries. Table 2.1 holds the final gross sample figures, the net samples (gross sample minus 'return to sender'), the number of returned questionnaires and the response rate per country. The response rate in column 4 is based on columns 2 and 3.

---

[1] European Foundation for the Improvement of Living and Working Conditions.

From the gross sample of 33,427 questionnaires, 845 (2.4 per cent) were returned to sender by the different postal services either because the address was wrong or unknown, the addressee had moved to an unknown address, or the company had ceased to exist altogether. By 15 November 1996, 5,786 questionnaires had been returned and it was on the basis of these that the data analysis took place. In data analysis the remaining sample distortions regarding sector and size of the workplace were weighted for each sector/size cell to reflect the original research universe. The sample distortions between countries were corrected by a weighting factor that accounted for the number of employees represented in the data set for each country and the overall size of the workplace in that country.

Assessment of the response

The number of explicit refusals was very low: only about 400 potential respondents indicated that they were not willing to cooperate. On the basis of remarks made by respondents either on the telephone or in the questionnaire, direct participation was regarded as a subject of some importance. In addition, a large number of respondents (47 per cent) responded positively to the question asking if they would like to receive a summary of the results.

Table 2.1 *Sample sizes and questionnaire returns*

	gross sample (absolute nos)	net sample (absolute nos)	questionnaire returns: (absolute nos)	response (%)
Denmark	2,600	2,535	674	26.6
France	5,028	4,870	598	12.3
Germany	4,954	4,887	826	16.9
Ireland	1,000	984	382	38.8
Italy	3,949	3,849	499	13.0
Netherlands	2,386	2,303	505	21.9
Portugal	1,000	996	298	29.9
Spain	5,062	4,872	460	9.4
Sweden	2,448	2,401	732	30.5
United Kingdom	5,000	4,881	812	16.6
Total	33,427	32,582	5,786	17.8

An overall return rate of 18 per cent was not as high as the Research Group hoped for. It is not out of line, however, with the only comparable cross-national survey of Price-Waterhouse-Cranfield (PWC) carried out in 1991 at company level. Like the EPOC survey, this was a postal survey. Its overall return rate of

Methodology: Static and Dynamic Dimensions of Gender

usable questionnaires was 17.1 per cent, which is almost identical to the EPOC response rate. Table 2.2 compares the results of the surveys in detail.

Table 2.2 *EPOC and Price-Waterhouse-Cranfield survey response rates*

	EPOC response rate %	PWC response rate %
Denmark	27	19
France	12	15
Germany	17	15
Ireland	39	(not in sample)
Italy	13	10
Netherlands	22	19
Portugal	30	(not in sample)
Spain	9	14
Sweden	31	42
United Kingdom	17	19
10 country average	18	17

(Price-Waterhouse-Cranfield: Switzerland 16%, Norway 28%)

It will be seen that the EPOC response rates for France, Spain, Sweden and the United Kingdom were below the PWC equivalents. Setting aside Ireland and Portugal, which were not included in the PWC study, the return rates of the remaining countries were higher in the EPOC survey.

Additional information from similar national surveys is also instructive:

– a German national postal survey on the same topic in the production sector had an identical response rate to that of the EPOC survey: 18 per cent (cf. ISI, 1996);
– an earlier Dutch national postal survey on a similar topic (Muffels, Heinen and van Mil, 1982) had a return rate of 28 per cent which is higher than that of the EPOC survey (22 per cent);
– the EPOC survey's response rate for Portugal (30 per cent) is very high. A similar postal survey carried out by Kovacs, Cerdeira and Moniz (1992) had a return rate of 12 per cent;
– high return rates seem to be the norm in Sweden. The EPOC rate for this country (31 per cent) is below that of the PWC survey (42 per cent), but it approaches the figure (34 per cent) of a recent national postal survey on flexible organisations (NUTEK, 1996).

Thus, the return rates for Germany, the Netherlands and Sweden were not out of line with what appears to be the norm for these countries. Taking the PWC study in addition, the rates for France, the United Kingdom and Spain in particular seem to be somewhat below expectations.

Comparable though it may be, an 18 per cent overall return rate raises the question of how far the estimated parameters of interest suffer from a probability bias. In other words, are the workplaces with direct participation underrepresented or overrepresented in the EPOC results? Are the data negatively or positively biased? This issue was investigated in a project undertaken by NUTEK, dealing with the spread and functioning of 'flexible organisations' in Sweden in preparation for the G7 summit in France in early summer 1996. The representative survey had a response rate of 34 per cent, which is very close to that of the EPOC survey for Sweden. To evaluate the representativity of the data, telephone follow-ups were made to try to establish the degree of flexibility in non-respondent organisations. The verdict was that, 'the non-response sample seems to have a larger proportion of workplaces defined as a flexible work organisation' as compared to the respondents (NUTEK, 1996, p.195; cf. also p.198). In other words, the survey results underestimated the extent of flexible organisations in Sweden.

It does not necessarily follow that the same is true of the EPOC results. It simply suggests that under-representation is a possibility, as is over-representation. There is no reason to believe that the EPOC results are biased one way or the other.

The concept of the largest occupational group

The EPOC survey targeted the largest occupational group (the 'largest number of non-managerial employees at this workplace' in the precise words of the questionnaire). This was done for two reasons: to reduce the complexity of answers required of respondents; and to ensure that answers were as characteristic of as many employees as possible. Inevitably, however, focusing on the largest occupational group (or LOG) raises questions about the relationship between these employees and the workforce as a whole. Especially important is whether or not it is possible to generalise from the experience of the LOG to the total workforce.

One feasibility study to ensure that the largest occupational group approximates to the workforce of the establishments is to correlate the number of employees within the LOG to the size of the whole workforce. Since the data set contains continuous values for both variables, Pearson's r can be used as a correlation measurement. In this case Pearson's r shows a value of .97 – which is significant at the .001 level – and indicates very clearly that the LOG can stand as a valid proxy for the workforce.

Methodological implications of adopting a gender perspective

The main two areas of focus of this report are the general characteristics of the survey workplaces and the gender dimensions of direct participation in those workplaces. In particular, the report examines the dimensions of direct participation in establishments with varying proportions of women in the largest occupational group.

A key question underlying this report therefore is: to what extent does the sex of employees affect their working conditions and their opportunities for participation in organisational change? In other words: in which circumstances does the sex of employees affect the dynamics of direct participation? The report draws upon the EPOC survey in order to address these questions. At this point, a major methodological constraint has to be acknowledged. The EPOC survey is an establishment-related survey. This means that the main unit of data collection and analysis is the establishment and its total workforce. The survey does not focus on individual employees or their interactions within establishments. Therefore, although we can identify the gender composition of the workforces of different establishments, we are not able to conduct any analysis of the circumstances of different groups of employees or individual workers. This poses problems in addressing questions relating to individual workplaces, for example, whether women are typically found in lower echelons of the survey organisations than men, or how social and interpersonal interactions reproduce structural inequality at workplace level. Yet these questions are important because they help us to find explanations for the continuing gender gap in organisations (Ridgeway, 1997). On the other hand, we are able to examine entire establishments, and this would not have been possible had the survey concentrated on individual employees. Indeed, as we shall see, there are a number of advantages deriving from establishment-based data for an analysis of gender segregation in working life.

Using the establishment as the basic unit of the analysis, then, our main hypotheses are that workplaces with a high proportion of female employees in the largest occupational group will show (1) other characteristics and (2) different dimensions of direct participation from those with lower proportions of women workers.

The EPOC survey respondents were asked to answer the questionnaire with respect to the largest group of employees working in non-managerial functions. As we have already noted, the largest occupational group (LOG) is a very solid approximation to the whole workforce. Therefore, referring to women in the LOG refers to women within the workforce of the establishment as a whole.

The major dimensions of the gender analysis

For the purposes of our analysis of gender and equal opportunities issues in direct participation and organisational change, two questions in the EPOC survey questionnaire are particularly important:

- 'What is the number of women in [the] Largest Occupational Group (LOG) of the establishment?'
- 'Has the composition of the largest occupational group been affected in the last three years by ... an increase in absolute number of women?'[2]

The first question asks for static information on the position of women within the survey establishments. The second asks for information on changes in their situation within the three years preceding the conduct of the survey. The dual nature of the data derived – both static and dynamic – is one of its the major defining characteristics.

The static dimension

Our main assumption here is that individual employees' work settings and conditions of employment, together with the opportunities for participation in organisational change which they enjoy, depend – among other things – on their sex. We can only examine this assumption by using workplace, i.e., establishment-based, data.

This generates our central hypothesis: as a consequence of the assumption above we expect to find that workplaces with a high proportion of female employees will have different characteristics and different dimensions of direct participation than workplaces with lower proportions of women. To operationalise this issue, we distinguish between four types of workplaces on the basis of what we call their 'gender composition':

- **Male only** establishments – those without women in the LOG. This does not mean that there are no women within the establishment as a whole, only that

---

[2] Questions cited from the original questionnaire.

there are no women within the largest group of employees (at which the EPOC survey questions were directed). These establishments have particular characteristics, as we will see in the next chapter. This means that they do not provide a very effective or useful comparative category.

- **Male-dominated** establishments – less than 33% of the LOG is female.
- **Mixed-sex** establishments – 34%-67% of the LOG is female.
- **Female-dominated** establishments – more than 68% of the LOG is female.

The distribution of establishments in the EPOC survey by their gender composition is shown below.

Table 2.3 *Distribution of establishments by proportion of women in the largest occupational group – 'gender composition'*

gender structure	percentage	total number
male-only	23	1,207
male-dominated	30	1,565
mixed	25	1,319
female-dominated	22	1,186
total	100	5,277

These types cover 5,277 cases or 91% of the questionnaires returned. More than half of the establishments (53%) reported no women or less than 33% women in their LOG. One in four establishments has a mixed-sex LOG and nearly 22% of all establishments are female-dominated. This latter category also includes establishments in which the LOG consists primarily of women (but these accounted for less than 4% of all establishments).

The dynamic dimension

In addition to a consideration of the structural features and direct participation practices of the different establishments within which women are employed, we also examine short-term changes in the numbers and proportions of women employed in these establishments. Here we use two kinds of variables:

- information about the increase in the absolute number of women within the LOG in the last three years[3];
- the feminisation or defeminisation of the establishments.

---

[3] The data do not contain any information about the reduction of the number of women.

As we have already noted, the proportion of women in the LOG is a good proxy for the proportion of women within the whole establishment. We therefore assume that a change in the proportion of women in the LOG represents a change in the proportion of women within the whole establishment. About 4,322 establishments (or 75% of the questionnaires returned) answered the survey question on the increase in the absolute number of women in the LOG.

Table 2.4 *Establishments of different gender compositions reporting changes in the number of women in the LOG*

increase reported in number of women	gender composition of establishment				
	male-only	male-dominated	mixed	female-dominated	average
yes	2	17	27	30	19
no	98	83	73	70	81
total	100	100	100	100	100
(n)	(921)	(1291)	(1062)	(863)	(4137)

About 20% of these establishments reported an increase in the absolute number of women. Table 2.4 shows that the four types of establishments varied in the extent to which they reported an increase in women in their LOG within the last three years. two per cent of the 'male-only' establishments reported an increase in the number of women, but these cases must be treated as inconsistencies in the data set. In 17% of the 'male-dominated' establishments, the number of women increased within the last three years. Thirty per cent of 'female-dominated' establishments and 27% of 'mixed-sex' establishments reported an increase in the employment of women. Of course, we would expect to see this: there must be a greater likelihood of such an increase in establishments which have a relatively high proportion of female employees to begin with. We look at the reasons for this in the next chapter.

However, we still have to put these changes in the context of changes in the absolute size of the whole workforce within the enterprise. As we only have information on the direction of changes in the total workforce size (not on the exact numerical value of that change), we can only make rough estimates of the degree of what we can refer to as 'feminisation', or otherwise, of the workforce. Table 2.5 below provides this estimate.

The first type of establishment we can single out is that in which women's share of total employment increased. Only in those cases where both an increase in the number of women in the LOG but *no* growth in the LOG as a whole has occurred, can we say with certainty that the *share* of women has increased, in other words, that the LOG has been 'feminised'. In all, 826 (or 19% of the questionnaires returned) of the establishments reported an increase in the number of women. In only 39% (30% + 9%) of these cases has the share of women increased. Overall, in only 6% of all the establishments in the survey has the share of women increased relative to the workforce as a whole.

Table 2.5 *Percentages of establishments which have increased the number of women in their workforces by percentages of those changing the number of employees in the LOG*

change in number of employees	increase in the number of women		
	yes	no	average
increased	61	27	33
same	30	41	39
reduced	9	32	27
total (n)	100 (826)	100 (3496)	100 (4322)

The second type of establishment of interest here is the type which has increased the number of employees overall but has not increased the number of women (938 respondents, representing 16% of the questionnaires returned).

Overall, we can identify three categories of establishments according to their dynamics of female employment:

- Establishments which have increased their employment of women, but have not changed the number of employees as a whole during the last three years. These establishments can be classified as **feminising establishments**, since the share of female workers in the whole workforce increased.
- Establishments which have increased their workforce but have not increased their employment of women. These establishments can be classified as **defeminising establishments** since the share of women in the workforce decreased.
- Establishments which (a) have neither increased the total number of employees nor the number of women, or (b) have increased both. For (a), there are three possible scenarios (and we are not able to tell which of the three applies). Either the number of employees has remained constant while the number of women has decreased (in which case they are 'defeminising' establishments); or no changes at all have taken place; or the number of

employees is reduced but the number of women has remained the same (in which case they are 'feminising' establishments). For (b), we do not know what the level of increase in either case has been, and therefore whether the proportion of women as a proportion of the total workforce has changed. We can therefore conclude nothing definite about the dynamics taking place in these establishments.

Table 2.6 *Feminisation and defeminisation of establishments in the EPOC survey*

	(n)	(%)
defeminisation	936	22
feminisation	320	7
indefinite	3064	71
total	4322	
percentage of the questionnaires returned:	75%	

Together with the information about the increase in the number of women, the classification above can be used to analyse the gender balance of the workforce. We can also relate the dynamics of 'feminisation' and 'defeminisation' to other relevant variables.

However, it is worth noting that 'feminisation' and 'defeminisation' are not the only indicators for the dynamics which we want to address in this report. In fact, as we have seen, 'feminising' establishments constitute only 6% of the survey questionnaires returned, and 39% of all establishments reporting an increase in the number of women. Similarly, 'defeminising' establishments relate to only 16% of the questionnaires returned and to 27% of those establishments which did not report an increase in the number of women. We therefore have no information on 53% of the questionnaires returned, and because of the small numbers involved in the remaining cases, this reduces the options for detailed analysis. Nevertheless, despite the small numbers, these are clear cases of changes in the gender balance of establishments, which allow us to make some important comments on gender segregation or gender equity in the survey establishments. For this reason, this issue is worth pursuing. However, we have to note that the data we are working with here are not necessarily representative of gender relations in establishments in society broadly. They are useful simply as **indicators** of trends which would have to be further investigated in other research.

Methodology: Static and Dynamic Dimensions of Gender

To verify our earlier speculative statement that we would expect establishments with a high proportion of women to be more likely to feminise, we now examine the gender composition of establishments which are feminising and defeminising.

Table 2.7 *Feminisation and the gender composition of establishments (percentages)*

gender dynamics of establishment	male-only	male-dominated	mixed-sex	female-dominated	average (n)
feminisation	1	7	11	10	7
defeminisation	30	25	18	15	22
indefinite	69	68	72	75	71
total	100	100	100	100	100
(n)	(883)	(1251)	(1015)	(839)	(3988)

This table shows us that there is little difference between establishments of different gender composition in each of the three categories – feminising, defeminising, and indefinite. However, if we confine the analysis simply to those establishments which clearly show either defeminisation or feminisation (N=1169), then there is a clear association between the gender structure of the establishments and the dynamics taking place within the workforce: male-dominated establishments are more likely to defeminise than other establishments, and workplaces which are female-dominated are more likely to feminise. Effectively, this constitutes an entrenchment of the gender segregation of these establishments. In Chapter 3 we will examine in more detail the form and nature of gender segregation there.

The remainder of this report

The rest of this report therefore uses three major variables in order to consider the gender dimensions of direct participation in the EPOC survey establishments:

- the static proportion of women within the largest occupational group of employees, which is taken as a proxy for the proportion of women within the establishment as a whole;
- the increase in the number of women within the last three years as a dynamic measure of the changing gender composition of the survey establishments;
- The feminisation or defeminisation of the survey establishments as a more specific dynamic of their gender composition.

Though the sex of an individual is almost always an independent variable in social surveys, the gender structure of an establishment, paradoxically and for several reasons, is not independent of other factors. The questions which we pose at particular points in the report determine the status of the variables presented above as dependent or independent. We are predominantly interested, however, in exploring factors which allow us to discriminate between different classes of establishments on the basis of their gender structure and gender dynamics, as these relate to direct participation.

Two qualifications concerning the data set are worth making at this point.

1) This is secondary analysis of a data set which was not specially designed for the analysis of gender segregation in establishments. Unfortunately, this means that we are unable to address issues such as sexual divisions of labour **within** establishments; the employment of women in particular occupational areas within establishments, or the patterns of interaction between bosses and subordinates, or between co-workers. These are, of course, issues of substantial relevance to a full understanding of women's employment and the conditions in which equal opportunities objectives can be pursued, and they deserve considerable attention in future research.

2) The data set contains only 18% of the establishments surveyed. A full methodological discussion of the response rate in the survey can be found in the main report of the survey, *New Forms of Work Organisation – Can Europe Realise its Potential?* (EFILWC, 1997).

With these caveats, the data reported here offers an instructive heuristic instrument with which to compare the gender dimensions of direct participation across different countries, sectors, and occupations. The comparative quality of the data is one its major advantages, and it is to a comparison of the features of the survey workplaces that we now turn[4].

---

[4] To preserve the readability of the main body of this report, we supply the measures of association and their level of significance in the Appendix.

References

European Foundation for the Improvement of Living and Working Conditions, *New forms of work organisation. Can Europe realise its potential, Results of a survey of direct employee participation in Europe*, Luxembourg, Office for Official Publications of the European Communities, 1997.

Fröhlich, D., Gill, C., and Krieger, H., European Foundation for the Improvement of Living and Working Conditions, *Workplace involvement in technological innovation in the European Community, Volume 1: Roads to Participation*, Luxembourg, Office for Official Publications of the European Communities, 1993.

Fröhlich, D. and Pekruhl, U., European Foundation for the Improvement of Living and Working Conditions, *Direct participation and organisational change – fashionable but misunderstood? An analysis of recent research in Europe*, Luxembourg, Office for Official Publications of the European Communities, 1996.

Geary, J. and Sisson, K., European Foundation for the Improvement of Living and Working Conditions, *Conceptualising direct participation in organisational change. The EPOC Project*, Luxembourg, Office for Official Publications of the European Communities, 1994.

Kovacs, I., Cerdeira, C. and Brandao Moniz, A., *Technological and Work Organisational Change in Portuguese Industry*, Lisbon, Programme PEDIP, 1992.

Lay, G., C. Dreher, and S. Kinkel, *Neue Produktionskonzepte leisten einen Beitrag zur Sicherung des Standorts Deutschland. Mitteilungen aus der Produktionsinnovationserhebung*, Karlsruhe, Fraunhofer Institut Systemtechnik und Innovationsforschung, Karlsruhe, Juli 1996.

Muffels, R., Heinen, T., and van Mil, G., *Werkoverleg en werkstructurering en de subsidieregeling arbeidsplaatsverbetering: En onderzoek bij bedrijven met meer dan 100 personeelsleden*, IVA, Tilburg, 1982.

NUTEK, *Towards Flexible Organisations*, Stockholm, NUTEK, 1996.

Price Waterhouse Cranfield Project on International Strategic Human Resource Management, Report, Cranfield, Cranfield School of Management, 1991.

Regalia, I., European Foundation for the Improvement of Living and Working Conditions, *Humanise work and increase profitability? Direct participation in organisational change viewed by the social partners in Europe,* Luxembourg, Office for Official Publications of the European Communities, 1995.

Ridgeway, Cecilia L., 'Interaction and the conservation of gender inequality: considering employment', *American Sociological Review*, Vol. 62, April 1997, pp. 218-235.

Chapter 3

Gender Dimensions of the Survey Workplaces

All forms of work reorganisation take place within the context of workplaces with particular characteristics. The processes and outcomes of direct participation can only be understood in the context of these characteristics. When assessing the equal opportunities dimensions of direct participation, the starting point must be an examination of the gender-related characteristics of workplaces, in other words, with gender divisions of labour, with gender segregation of work, with the relative positions of men and women in the various establishments. This chapter discusses some conceptual tools which will help us to do that. It begins by outlining the concept of 'gender structure', and shows how the concept has been operationalised for the purposes of this analysis. It discusses the workplaces in the survey in terms of various characteristics: industry sector, largest occupational group, working time patterns of largest occupational group, and ownership of firm, as differentiated by their gender structures. In this way, the chapter aims to set the scene for the later analysis of gender patterns in direct participation which follow in this report.

The concept of 'gender structure'

In analyses of organisational changes, including the practice of direct participation, it always has to be remembered that the workforce has two sexes. Many discussions of industrial, organisational and technological change make the mistake of assuming that the dynamics of work in areas where men are employed are the dynamics of work operating for all employees. Yet there is ample evidence to show that men and women inhabit very different areas of industrial and organisational life, and have very different experiences of processes of change. These differences warrant a gender-differentiated analysis of organisations and their key dynamics. If we are really to make meaningful statements about employee participation, or to develop effective equal opportunities policies, then we have to be alive to the different spheres in which male and female employees find themselves.

It is now a commonplace that, in advanced industrial societies, men and women are largely segregated from one another in the occupations which they do. It is also true that men find access to a much greater range of occupational groups than do women, who are found working within a relatively narrow range of occupational areas. This separation of women from men at work, and their simultaneous exclusion from a number of areas of work, has been described by the concept of occupational segregation (Hakim, 1979).

Women are concentrated in particular industries and sectors – health, education, public administration, financial services, retailing, textiles, garment production, and in the lower echelons of manufacturing firms. They are largely absent from other industry sectors: construction, defence, mechanical engineering and mining, for example. They are also concentrated at the lower end of occupational hierarchies – vertically as well as horizontally segregated. They are strongly represented in low-grade or low-paid jobs in the services industries (as clerks, customer service assistants, checkout operators, call centre operators, telephonists, nurses, orderlies, ancillary staff, teachers). In manufacturing, they dominate semiskilled and unskilled areas like assembly work, routine testing, and packaging. The great majority of women work almost entirely with other women, few entering into male-dominated spheres of work. The persistent wages and skills gap between the two sexes in the workforce is in part a function of this continuing gender segregation.

The differential between men's and women's position in the labour market is the product of both material and cultural factors which operate not only within the labour market itself but also beyond it, in the domestic sphere, in the education and training system, in the state and its systems of social protection and employment legislation, and so on. For example, the level of widespread and affordable childcare provision shapes women's access to employment, as do dominant notions of the acceptability of women working. Similarly, their access to certain forms of education shapes the types of jobs which they can take up, as do cultural definitions of the skills which women typically possess. Women's access to certain areas of work in turn conditions their access to training and their ability to progress within organisations and exploit new opportunities. Sex-typing of occupations such as secretarial work or nursing also contributes to the occupational segregation of women; cultural processes have historically allocated women to these areas of work, but contemporary technological and organisational developments may serve to undermine this association. At state level, systems of social protection or employment legislation – for example in relation to part-time work – also affect the diffusion and take-up of such employment.

Gender divisions are therefore a consequence of both labour-demand and labour-supply behaviour, and they are, of course, both enduring and dynamic. There are many intersecting structural and cultural factors at work shaping women's labour market position and labour process experiences, and these are constantly being created and recreated, dismantled and remantled, through individual and collective action. We are convinced that women's overall labour market position is, in turn, a key factor shaping their relationship to direct participation. The types of jobs which women do and the types of establishments in which they are employed are surely directly linked to women's access to, role in, and experiences of direct participation in organisational change. The purpose of this report, and in particular of this chapter in the report, is therefore to further our understanding of the dynamics of direct employee participation by women *in the context of* their position in labour markets, in firms and organisations, and in trade unions and related bodies. We know that the issue of gender matters in these contexts, and this report aims to give this point some substance in relation to the particular establishments studied in this survey. Our approach to the gender and direct participation issue is a dual one. First, we believe that access to direct participation may be gendered, that is, that men and women, by virtue of their differential labour market positions, will have unequal opportunities to engage in direct participation. We address this issue in Chapters 4 and 5. Second, we believe that the outcomes of direct participation will be different for the two sexes in the workforce, and we consider the implications for equal opportunities in Chapter 6.

A useful way of conceptualising the gendered context for the practice of direct participation is via the notion of the 'gender structure' of workplaces. This is a concept which seeks to describe the sexual division of labour within the organisations surveyed, and to reveal the position, meaning and dynamics of women's work within these organisations. It has its antecedents in the writings of Sandra Harding (1986), who has proposed three aspects of gender which can help to conceptualise the workings of gender relations between women and men: individual gender, symbolic gender and the division of labour by gender. It is with the third (and to some extent with the second) of these three aspects of gender that we are concerned in this report. Although Harding's concept refers to the gendered division of labour in society broadly, in paid work but also in unpaid work and in other social activities, we are concerned here with the structural differences between men and women in employment and at work, and in their relationships to direct participation.

Yvonne Hirdman (1988) has developed the concept of a 'gender system' to denote the consistent segregation, disadvantaging and devaluing of women in all areas of social life. Sundin (1995) has elaborated this concept in relation to working life: the gender system conditions both the material and the cultural characteristics of women's and men's work. There is a 'gender order' to occupational structures: occupations carry 'gender labels' which define them as masculine or feminine, and which are constructed under 'gender regimes' within particular organisations. An example of a gender regime and its workings might be found in an office, in which men are found in management positions and women are primarily employed in subordinate roles, as secretarial and clerical staff. However, a gender regime can equally give rise to a workplace like an oil rig or a construction site, in which the work is male-dominated, the workforce is perhaps strongly unionised, and the interrelationships between men are central to the culture of the workplace. A gender regime can also denote a female-dominated workplace, such as a call centre or a typing pool, in which particular social and gender identities are forged among the women, and in which the supervisory function carries a particular class and gender label.

There is a growing body of literature which is concerned with addressing the almost total absence of attention to gender and gender systems within discussions of organisational transformation, and with understanding ways in which such transformation might be used as an opportunity to challenge existing gender systems in European workplaces (Goldmann et al, 1994; Gunnarsson, 1994; Goldmann, 1995; Shapiro and Austin, 1996; Gratton, 1997). Here, equal opportunities and organisational change issues have for the first time been brought together, and the benefits of addressing the two sets of issues in tandem are articulated. In this body of literature, equal opportunities concerns are no longer the sole preserve of personnel or human resources managers, or indeed equal opportunities officers, in organisations. Rather, equal opportunities is a mainstream issue bearing fundamentally upon the entire efficient management of the organisation, a strategic and business issue rather than simply an ethical one (Goldmann, 1995; Shapiro and Austin, 1996).

In this conception, moves away from centralised, hierarchical, rigid, gender-segregated, Taylorist, and fragmented forms of work organisation are seen as having important equal opportunities implications along many dimensions. However, potentially positive outcomes are much more likely to be achieved when new methods of work organisation are developed within the context of a truly innovative strategy for enhanced organisational flexibility and product quality rather than within a somewhat conventional approach which simply concentrates on cost reduction (Lay, 1997).

Several aspects of new forms of working have been identified as potentially beneficial for female workers and for equal opportunities more broadly. Innovations in working time have been introduced across many economic sectors in conjunction with new forms of work organisation, involving working time arrangements which do not centre on the conventional full-time model. Indeed, the creation of increasing numbers of part-time, temporary and subcontracted jobs throughout Europe has been one of the most noteworthy developments in work organisation in the 1990s. In equal opportunities terms, these developments have been primarily negative to date. Women have been particularly affected by the increase in part-time employment, which for the most part has simply exacerbated the 'casualisation' of their work and worsened their access to training and employee development prospects. However, alternative approaches to employment flexibility which do not rest on cost-cutting imperatives emphasise the potential for improved control over their lives that flexible working time affords employees. This is particularly critical for women who invariably have to balance paid employment with domestic labour, and especially childcare or care of elderly relatives. Working time flexibility, if organised in an employee-centred way, could conceivably release women from the trap of having to settle for insecure and poorly paid employment in order to manage their domestic demands (European Parliament, 1996; Meulders and Plasman, 1996; Marin, 1996).

In terms of work processes, total quality management has been identified as a vehicle by which gender equity can be achieved in organisations while they simultaneously pursue strategic organisational improvements. If implemented systematically and in a thorough-going manner, total quality management allows the full involvement of all employees and the full use of their skills and abilities in the project of enhancing organisational performance for competitive advantage (Shapiro and Austin, 1996). Shapiro and Austin identify a strategy which could be built on total quality management, which they label 'Equality Driven Total Quality'. Both strategies, however, require four essential organisational pillars: information sharing and communication, knowledge and skills development through training, rewards for employees, and empowerment of employees through the diffusion of decision-taking authority downwards through organisations.

In studies of new organisational forms in implementation, Goldmann (1995) notes that 'qualified groupwork' is potentially positive for female employees. Here again, if groupwork is to have gender equitable outcomes, there are prerequisites to be achieved which parallel those in the Equality Driven Total Quality model. Groupwork must be organised on the basis of function and task integration, self-regulation and self-control, cooperation and communication, and qualification integration (Seitz, 1993). Even without these prerequisites, however, groupwork has been found to reduce gender hierarchies in organisations and to allow relative improvements in the position, earnings and job satisfaction of women, both in manufacturing and in services. To some extent in these settings, men undertake tasks previously carried out only by women, while women take on 'men's work', and thus the gender system of activities is partly reshaped; but equally, many tasks continue to be assigned not according to objective prerequisites or qualification but according to pre-existing gender labels. With the flattening of hierarchies, women gain access, for the first time in some cases, to simple leadership roles, like the role of group speaker. Moreover, they have fewer organisational layers and obstacles to negotiate in moving into more senior positions (Gunnarsson, 1994). They also gain access to advanced training programmes in order to develop both technical skills and social competencies for autonomous working. Organisational and competitive advantages accrue: as their opportunities improve and professional perspectives develop, women become much more active participants in innovation processes (Goldmann, 1995).

The emphasis on multiskilling and particularly the reliance on social skills in teamworking and groupworking is often held up as potentially advantageous for women. It is commonly argued that women possess social, interpersonal and communications skills in abundance and are therefore particularly well suited to work and progress in organisations where these skills are critical. There is some evidence of women benefiting from the emphasis which many organisations now place on social skills, particularly where improvements in customer service are involved. For example, in the banking industry, where in the past women were confined largely to routine clerical functions and bank management was a 'gentlemanly' occupation, new opportunities for women to move into management functions have become apparent (Crompton and Sanderson, 1990). On the other hand, in the context of flatter organisations themselves, working in retail banking is becoming increasingly routinised and the possibilities for progress within them are diminishing. Moreover, essentialist assumptions that women are the 'natural' bearers of social skills do not necessarily promote equal opportunities objectives; they may simply serve to fix women into gender-stereotyped areas of work and these skills can become so taken-for-granted in women that they are paradoxically not rewarded when used by them (Poynton, 1993; Woodfield, 1994).

Overall, many accounts of contemporary organisational innovation stress the fact that future competitive advantage will depend upon organisations developing their own internal creativity and learning, and that employees, far from being costs to be reduced, will be resources at the centre of organisational learning strategies. If human labour is to be re-evaluated in this way, then female labour must also be reassessed and reoriented, possibly in a paradigmatic change from the past (Moldaschl, 1992). Almost without exception, the work, knowledge and expertise of women employees has up to now been undervalued, downgraded, underpaid and underpromoted. Whether employee participation will provide the vehicle by which gender inequalities at work can be addressed and transcended is a major issue confronting organisational managements and equal opportunities specialists alike, and to provide some initial answers to this question constitutes the central concern of this report.

Operationalising 'gender structures' in the EPOC survey

The occupational and hierarchical positions of employees within organisations, and their potential to benefit from organisational change programmes, all depend strongly upon the gender structures of those organisations. In order to operationalise these ideas within the context of the EPOC survey data, we have developed a variable which we presented in Chapter 2, and which represents the gender composition of the organisations in the survey. This variable allows us to examine the patterns of work organisation and employee participation within establishments – their gender structures. To recap, we can now distinguish between workplaces with different gender compositions, and we show again in Figure 3.1 how the EPOC survey workplaces are distributed. The different categories of establishment are:

- establishments with women totally absent from the largest occupational group (LOG) – which we designate **male-only**;
- establishments with women constituting less than 33% of the members of the largest occupational group – we call these **male-dominated**;
- establishments with a gender mix in the largest occupational group and between 34% and 67% of its members being female – we call these establishments **mixed-sex**; and
- establishments in which the largest occupational group is made up of more than 68% women, which we have labelled **female-dominated**.

Figure 3.1 *Proportion of establishments by share of women in the largest occupational group*

female-dominated 22%
male-only 23%
mixed 25%
male-dominated 30%

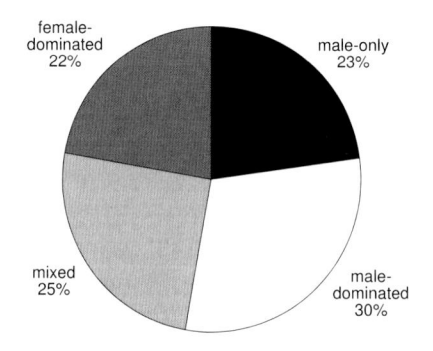

Figure 3.1 shows the percentage of establishments in each category of gender composition. There is very little difference in the proportion of establishments in each group. However, it is worth noting that the survey is slightly biased in favour of male-dominated and men-only establishments and this confirms the division of labour in society at large. In other words, while 23% of the organisations surveyed were male only, a smaller proportion – 22% – was female-dominated, and by implication a lesser proportion (7.7%) were female-only.

We expect workplaces with a high proportion of women to show certain other characteristics. First, we expect gender composition and gender structure to be strongly related to industry sector and to the occupation of the LOG, given that we know that strong occupational segregation by sex operates in European workplaces. We examine these associations below. Second, we expect workplaces where women form a large proportion of the workforce to display further features of what is often thought of as 'typical women's work'. In particular, they are likely to have a relatively large and growing proportion of part-time workers compared to male-dominated workplaces; evidence from other studies shows that part-time work is growing as a form of employment across the EU, particularly in areas where women are employed (Beatson, 1995; Rubery, Smith and Fagan, 1995; Neathey and Hurstfield, 1995). Part-time contracts are an increasingly significant form of employment in retailing, in financial services, in education, and in healthcare – all areas in which women are strongly represented. By contrast, temporary contracts are much more likely to be taken up by male members of the workforce. We consider the reasons for this in more detail below.

Analysis of workplaces by gender might also be expected to show differences in the labour processes of the main occupational groups. If women are segregated in the lower echelons of their occupations, then we might expect their jobs to be more repetitive and less complex than those in male-dominated workplaces. The focus of this survey is on the extent of organisational change – including flexibility at work – taking place in European workplaces and the direct participation practices surrounding such change. To what extent do female employees now have flexible working patterns? Do they remain segregated in the more routine areas of employment, where historically they have been concentrated?

Given, in addition, the relatively low costs to employers of employing women – women continue to earn an average of 75% of what men earn across the EU – another hypothesis we can make is that male-only or male-dominated workplaces might be more capital-intensive than female ones, as employers seek to displace their higher-priced labour power through the use of technologies. Historical evidence of technical change over the past 200 years points to the fact that priority areas for mechanisation and automation have been where labour power is relatively expensive (see for example, Landes, 1969; Cockburn, 1985; Webster, 1990; Freeman and Soete 1994).

Third, we know that women are in general less strongly unionised than their male counterparts. In part, this is a function of the industry sectors in which they work. Services industries, retailing, financial services and private sector clerical work are all sectors which are traditionally much less strongly unionised than the manufacturing and extraction industries in which men have been employed. Though this occupational segregation by sectors is to some extent being undermined by the current decline of heavy manufacturing and mining industries in parts of the EU, nevertheless a pattern of unionisation by sex has been established by this sectoral segregation of the sexes. The industries which have historically been strongly unionised are those in which men have been employed and from which women have been largely absent: mining, mechanical engineering, automotive industry, printing, electrical engineering and transport. Women's poorer access to unions is also a reflection of the fact that some employers in industries where women do work have pursued conscious strategies to develop parallel or alternative structures to trade unions, such as the staff associations established by firms within the financial services sector. In other industries where women work, in particular in the retailing sector, employers have preferred not to recognise trade unions at all, and indeed workplaces with non-union agreements are a growing phenomenon in some countries, such as the UK and Ireland. But even in areas where trade unions do represent women workers, their representation has been poor, with few women participating actively or being fully enfranchised in trade union agendas for action (West, 1982; Cockburn, 1991).

The extent to which access to direct participation is linked to access to trade unionism is ascertained when we discuss the gender dimensions of direct participation in the next chapter. On the basis of all these aspects of women's employment, however, we would expect to see a marked gender difference in direct participation patterns across workplaces, both in terms of the workplace dynamics themselves and in terms of the differential access of men and women within those workplaces to direct participation. This is the subject of the rest of this report. First, however, we offer an analysis by gender of the workplaces surveyed and we highlight some of the ways in which they are differentiated from one another along gender lines.

The gender structure of the establishments surveyed

Key findings

- In more than half of the establishments in the survey, women were either absent or in a small minority in the largest occupational group.
- More than one third of establishments increasing their number of women are mixed-sex establishments to start with. Female-dominated establishments are in fact less likely to increase the number of women they employ.
- Establishments with a strong female presence are mainly public and private personal service sector establishments. Their main activities are in health, education, social care, public administration and commercial services.

Gender Dimensions of the Survey Workplaces

Figure 3.1 indicates that more than half of the establishments surveyed had no women, or less than 33% women, in their largest occupational group, whilst only 22.5% of workplaces had no or less than 32% men in that group. This is an imbalance in the labour force participation of women and men in the establishments surveyed, and illustrates an inequality in labour market participation which, though declining, continues to exist in European society at large. However, not all member countries have the same patterns of labour market participation by women and men; historically the northern European countries, and particularly the Nordic countries, have relatively high rates of female labour market participation and, also, relatively advanced systems of social protection and childcare support for their female workers. Denmark, Sweden and Norway all have almost equal participation by women and men, while in Finland there has been equal participation for many years. This has been facilitated by systems of social protection which do not discriminate against women who work part time, and this contributes to their overall participation rate in the labour market in those countries. Culturally, too, Scandinavian women have not been inhibited from working in the ways that they have elsewhere. In the mid-European and particularly in the southern European countries, by contrast, there have been both structural and cultural obstacles to women's labour market participation. Though this is now changing rapidly, in some sectors in some countries, such as the financial services in Spain, women are still newcomers to the labour force.

Table 3.1 *Distribution of the establishments by gender composition and country*

country	male-only	male-dominated	mixed	female-dominated	total (n)
DK	23	36	20	21	100 (604)
FRA	28	17	25	29	100 (566)
GER	18	30	27	25	100 (755)
IRL	22	27	29	22	100 (362)
ITA	28	42	21	10	100 (452)
NL	26	34	16	24	100 (462)
POR	38	30	20	13	100 (255)
SPA	20	34	23	24	100 (399)
SWE	20	29	22	29	100 (707)
UK	18	29	29	24	100 (735)
average	23	30	24	23	100
(n)	(1233)	(1600)	(1264)	(1200)	(5297)

Table 3.1 shows the country distribution of the establishments by their gender composition. There are high proportions of mixed-sex establishments in Germany, Ireland, and the UK, while Sweden has an equal balance of male-dominated and female-dominated establishments. France, on the other hand, has comparatively segregated establishments: the greatest proportions of workplaces there are either male-only or female-dominated. Italy and Portugal have particularly strongly male workplaces: the highest proportions of establishments in those countries are either male-only or male-dominated. These figures bear out our general knowledge of country differences in male and female labour market participation: the labour market participation rate for women is lower in the Latin countries than in their northern European counterparts. More surprising is the fact that in the Spanish and Dutch establishments in this survey, the same proportions are male-dominated workplaces (34% of all workplaces in each country) and the same are female-dominated (24% in each country). Moreover, there is a larger proportion of mixed sex establishments in Spain than in the Netherlands. These figures do not follow gender patterns of labour market participation which we know to prevail in these countries in general, and which suggest a much higher rate of female labour market participation in the Netherlands than is shown here. Our figures may be distorted by the relatively small size of the survey sample, particularly when disaggregated by country[1].

Table 3.2 *Gender composition of establishments by whether they have increased the number of women in their largest occupational group*

number of women increased	male-only	male-dominated	mixed	female-dominated	total (n)
yes	17	28	37	21	100 (789)
no	27	32	22	18	100 (3348)
average	22	31	26	21	100 (4137)

Table 3.2 shows which establishments reported an increase in the number of women in their largest occupational group. It has been calculated on the basis of the same data as in Table 2.4, but it presents this data in a slightly different way, to emphasise the gender distribution of establishments increasing their female workforces compared with those not increasing their female workforces.

---

[1] We have not found any association between the size of the establishments and their gender composition which is worth reporting (see Table 3A1 in the Appendix).

Gender Dimensions of the Survey Workplaces

Overall, we see that numerically, many more workplaces – even those which are already highly feminised – reported no increase in women's participation in their labour forces than those that did report an increase. However, establishments of mixed sex have the highest share of those which report an increase in their employment of women – a higher share than sexually segregated establishments (male and female-dominated ones) and a much higher share than male-only workplaces. (It is not clear why the share of male-dominated establishments to take on more women is larger than that of female-dominated ones.) Could this represent the decline of the sexual division of labour in these establishments? To answer this question, we would need to know more about the establishments in question and their basic characteristics. What occupational groups and what types of work are involved? In which industry sectors are they found, and are these innovating types of organisations? In the following chapters, we examine the types of innovations being put in place in the survey establishments, and consider the effects of these innovations on the sexual division of labour. The variables of 'feminisation' and 'de-feminisation', which we discussed in Chapter 2, will also help us to assess these possible developments; we look at the EPOC survey establishments from this perspective later in this and in subsequent chapters.

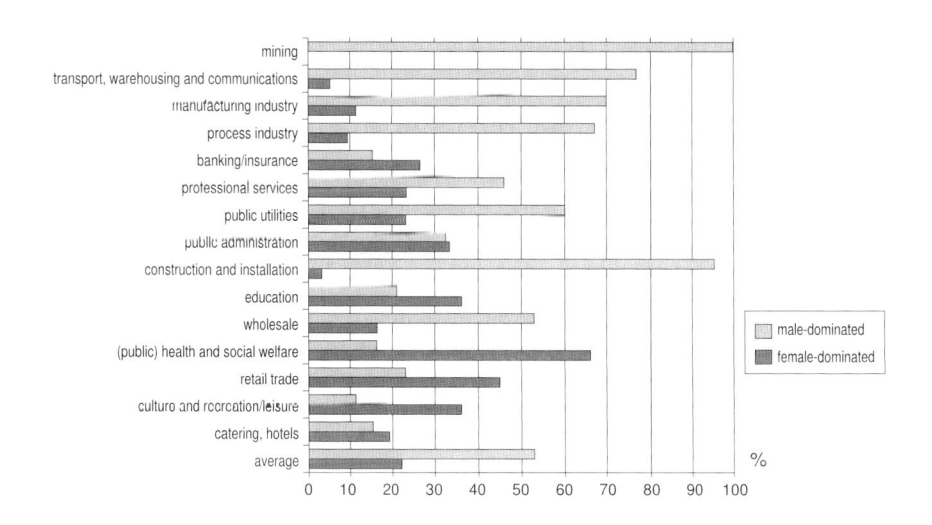

Figure 3.2 *Gender composition of establishments by sector*

Figure 3.2 shows how the gender structure of the survey establishments relates to industry sector. It illustrates the segregation of women and men in the EPOC survey in different areas of the economy. Women are, as we expected, absent from mining and construction, and are thinly represented in transport, manufacturing and public utilities. They are, however, more numerous in banking and insurance, professional services, public administration, education, culture/recreation and catering and hotels. They are very dominant in the workforces in public administration, education, health, retail, and culture/recreation – in other words, in the public sector or personal services areas of the private sector. Women's concentration in particular sectors and their absence from others may well be critical for their overall access to direct participation, for we know that the practice of direct participation varies greatly by industry sector. We look at this question in Chapter 4.

Table 3.3 *Gender composition of establishments by occupation of largest occupational group (as percentage of all establishments in each occupational group)*

	\multicolumn{4}{c}{gender composition of establishment}	
occupational group	male-only	male-dominated	mixed	female-dominated	total (n)
production; operational	34	36	20	10	100 (2136)
commercial; sales; marketing	5	28	33	35	100 (708)
medical; social care	6	5	19	70	100 (216)
transport; warehousing; distribution	36	42	11	10	100 (279)
educational	1	13	41	45	100 (227)
personal services; catering	3	15	42	39	100 (205)
administrative; clerical	3	11	48	38	100 (441)
repair and maintenance	39	39	22	0	100 (117)
technical	34	51	12	4	100 (295)
average	23	30	25	22	100 (4892)

Examination of occupational areas in which women work bears out this analysis. As Table 3.3 shows, establishments which are female-dominated are most likely to have workforces in medical, social care and educational jobs, and in commercial, sales and marketing, personal services and administrative functions. Male-dominated establishments, by contrast, are more likely to have workforces concerned with production, transport, warehousing, repair and maintenance, and technical occupations. This table, then, illustrates the concept of 'occupational segregation by sex', and suggests that if direct participation is differentiated by occupation then it will be gender differentiated by implication.

Table 3.4 *Feminisation and masculinisation of establishments by occupational group*

dominant occupational group of establishment	establishments in which women are increasing as a proportion of the total workforce	establishments in which men are increasing as a proportion of the total workforce	Total (n)
production/transport	13	87	100 (558)
commercial/personal services	29	71	100 (230)
medical/education/ administration	49	51	100 (200)
repair/technical	25	75	100 (98)
average	24	76	100 (1086)

Table 3.4 suggests that the EPOC survey establishments are not increasing their share of women. Indeed this finding runs contrary to those of more widescale employment surveys which show women to be the principal beneficiaries of employment growth (at the expense of young unskilled men). The EPOC survey establishments, by contrast, are more likely to 'masculinise' their workforces[2]. This is strongly true in already male-dominated occupations in production and transport, and in technical areas of work, but it is also true in more female-dominated occupations such as nursing, teaching, and clerical work. Although just under half of the survey establishments employing medical staff, educationalists or administrative staff – 'feminine' jobs – are feminising their labour forces, we are still left with the question of whether women are really benefiting significantly from employment changes or new job creation in the survey establishments. The data indicate that they are not, contrary to wider notions about women being the key beneficiaries of employment restructuring in Europe. It may be, however, that women do 'benefit' from particular employment arrangements – i.e. from the creation of particular *types* of employment, such as part-time employment. To consider the gender dimension of what is often regarded as 'non-standard' employment, we now turn to an examination of increases in part-time and temporary work in the EPOC establishments.

---

[2] It should be noted that this discrepancy arises from the fact that the EPOC survey was conducted at the level of establishments, unlike other surveys which are generally conducted at the level of the labour market as a whole. Although the majority of EPOC establishments have increased their proportion of male employees, we have no information on how significant these increases are in the context of wider employment change. The results of other employment surveys suggest that they are not typical.

Gender differences in working conditions and in employment contracts

Key findings
- 'Atypical' employment is very strongly gendered in the survey workplaces, with female-dominated workplaces particularly tending to increase their part-time labour forces and male-dominated workplaces increasing temporary work.
- 'Atypical' employment developments also vary by industry sector, with particular sectors most likely to increase part-time employment. Over half of retailing establishments in the survey increased their use of part-time employees.

The survey results show very clearly that the form of employment contract is a gendered aspect of work. It also confirms the results of other research which indicate that different forms of 'casual' employment contract – for example, part-time contracts, temporary contract, self-employment and outsourcing – are differentially distributed between the two sexes.

Figure 3.3 *Gender composition of establishments reporting an increase in part-time and temporary employment contracts*

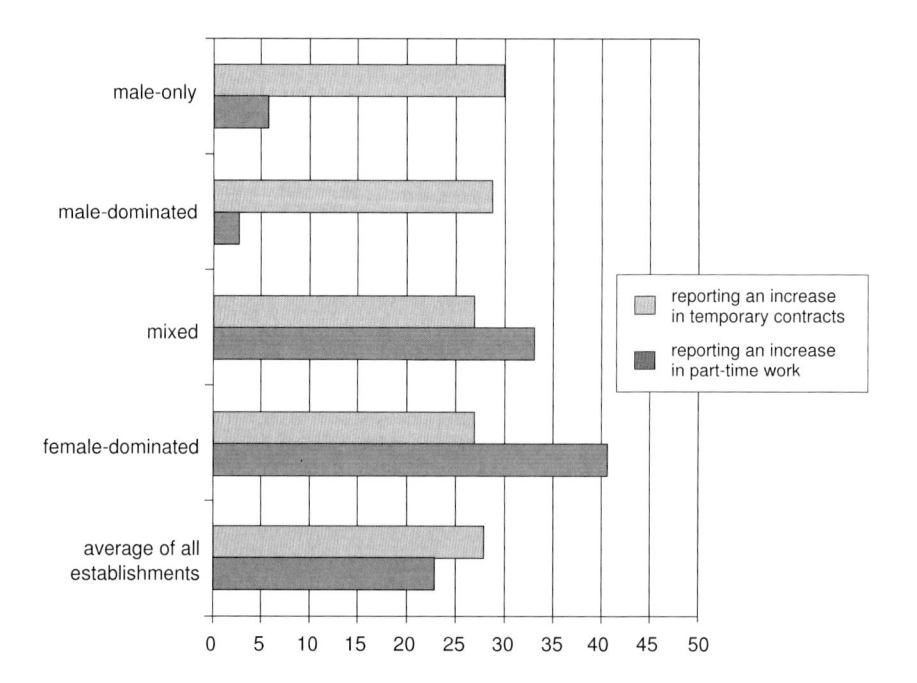

Figure 3.3 shows how 'atypical' working has increased over the past three years and how this is related to the gender structure of the establishments surveyed. Of female-dominated workplaces, 43.1% report an increase in part-time contracts; 32.5% (or one-third) of mixed workplaces do the same. Around 29% of workplaces report an increase in temporary contracts regardless of their gender structure. The increase in temporary contracts is greater overall than that of part-time work, but in female-dominated work, by far the most important growth is in part-time work.

This confirms what existing literature tells us about the flexibilisation, or casualisation, of work: namely, that it is gender-differentiated. Part-time work is an increasingly important feature of women's employment: it is used in industries where women are central to the labour force – in retailing, financial services, and education, for example. Temporary contracts are much more characteristic of men's jobs, and indeed men take up such contracts for different reasons than those which impel women into part-time work. Sometimes they become self-employed or temporarily employed upon being made redundant from large firms. Sometimes, as in the IT or telecommunications industries, they become subcontractors on temporary contracts to their former employers (BIPE Conseil, 1996). (Casual work is therefore to some extent a feature of particular economic sectors.) Indeed, it is worth noting that part-time work is, in many countries, offered to and taken up by women precisely because it allows them to combine paid work with domestic responsibilities. Country differences in women's part-time working patterns are strongly related to childcare regimes and school hours (Rubery et al, 1995; European Commission, 1996). To what extent developments in flexible working are linked to direct participation – in other words, are part and parcel of wider programmes of organisational change – will be examined in Chapter 4.

Figure 3.4 shows that in the EPOC survey, the increased use of part-time work was highly variable across countries, with the highest increases recorded in Sweden, the UK and France. In Sweden, part-time working has always been relatively high, and in addition, recent welfare expenditure cuts may be reducing the state provision of childcare and thereby placing women under pressure to work part-time. In the UK, the deregulation of labour markets during the 1980s and early 1990s has created considerable employer demand for part-time labour in particular sectors (most notably the retail sector), though with new part-time employee protection in place, it remains to be seen whether this trend will continue. The southern European countries, by contrast, show relatively low increases in part-time employment; indeed, part-time working is in general less a feature of their employment environment, and women's labour market participation in general is comparatively low.

Figure 3.4 *Proportions of establishments in each country which have increased part-time employment*

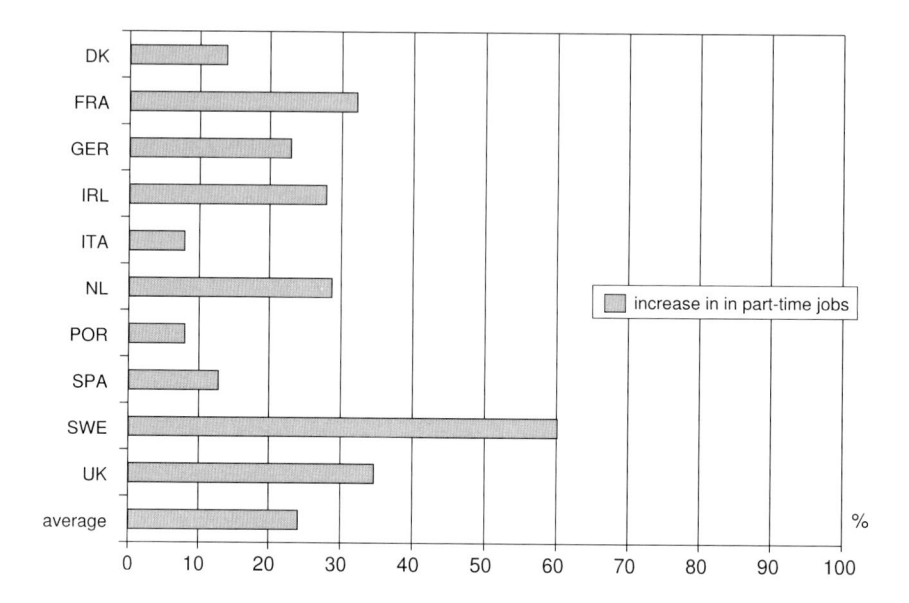

Country	increase in part-time jobs (%)
DK	~13
FRA	~33
GER	~23
IRL	~35
ITA	~10
NL	~30
POR	~5
SPA	~13
SWE	~62
UK	~37
average	~25

Tables 3.5 and 3.6 show the gender dimension of different forms of employment flexibility. Table 3.5 indicates that although the bulk of establishments in the survey did not increase their use of part-time contracts, those which did were more than twice as likely to be establishments which were also feminising their labour forces as to be establishments which were not. Similarly and conversely, Table 3.6 indicates that most establishments did not increase their use of temporary contracts, but those that did so were slightly likely to be establishments which were *not* feminising (though the difference here cannot be taken to be significant). Trends towards greater use of part-time workers, in other words, are associated with increasing proportions of female labour; while trends towards greater use of temporary contracts are not so associated (because temporary contracts are more used in 'male' areas of work)[3].

---

[3] Additional information on the association between the increase in the number of women and the increase in part-time work and in temporary work is included in the Appendix (Tables 3A2 and 3A3).

Table 3.5 *Part-time work increase and feminisation of establishments*

	feminisation of the workforce		
changes in part-time work	feminisation	no feminisation	average (n)
increase	39	15	20
no increase	61	85	80
all (n)	100 (253)	100 (900)	100 (1153)

Table 3.6 *Temporary work increase and feminisation of establishments*

	feminisation of the workforce		
changes in temporary contracts	feminisation	no feminisation	average
increase	27	29	28
no increase	73	71	72
all (n)	100 (219)	100 (910)	100 (1129)

The gender dimension of employment flexibility can be further illustrated by distinguishing between the different industry sectors which are moving towards greater employment flexibility through part-time working.

Table 3.7 *Part-time work increase by industry sector of establishments*

	changes in part-time jobs		
industry sector	increase	no increase	total (n)
mining	0	100	100 (23)
transport, warehousing and communications	18	82	100 (192)
manufacturing industry	12	88	100 (1470)
process industry	9	91	100 (292)
banking/insurance	20	80	100 (79)
professional services	21	79	100 (317)
public utilities	28	72	100 (122)
public administration	33	67	100 (337)
construction and installation	7	93	100 (310)
education	28	72	100 (187)
wholesale	22	78	100 (437)
(public) health/social welfare	46	54	100 (288)
retail trade	51	49	100 (576)
culture and recreation/leisure	48	52	100 (61)
catering, hotels	42	58	100 (83)
average	24	76	100 (4774)

In Table 3.7, we see that those industry sectors with the greatest proportions of establishments increasing part-time work are those in which women are most strongly represented – retailing; the leisure industries; hotels and catering, and public administration among them. Equally, traditionally male-dominated industries show little or no increases in part-time working – this is the case in mining, construction, process industries and manufacturing industries. We are now beginning to build up a picture of the types of organisations which are introducing changes in their employment arrangements. The important issue for consideration in subsequent chapters is whether these changes are being pursued as part of a coherent programme of organisational change, whether they are linked to direct participation, and what this means for their female employees and for equal opportunities in general.

Company ownership

Table 3.8 *Gender composition of establishment by ownership and orientation to profit-making*

ownership and orientation to profit-making	male-only	male-dominated	mixed	female-dominated	total
privately-owned and profit-making	27	32	24	18	100 (3635)
privately-owned and non profit-making	14	23	23	40	100 (389)
publicly-owned and profit-making	30	30	26	14	100 (133)
publicly-owned and non profit-making	7	21	36	36	100 (623)
average	23	30	25	22	100 (4780)

Table 3.8 examines the gender composition of the establishments in the survey in terms of their ownership and orientation to profit-making. There are some clear gender divisions here: more than half the companies which are privately owned and profit oriented are male-dominated or male-only (58.8% in total). This is probably an industry sector effect; table 3A4 in the Appendix shows that nearly half of private profit-making companies are industrial, and we know that, with some notable exceptions (such as textiles and garment production), industrial organisations are male-dominated and male-only.

The public profit-making companies in the survey are also male-dominated or male only (60.2%), and this too reflects their sector – one third of public profit-making companies are in the industrial or construction sectors, the latter of which is not a female-friendly area of work. On the other hand, women dominate employment in about 40% of the companies which are privately-owned but non profit-making, and, unexpectedly, are more dominant there than in public non profit-making organisations. This suggests that they are most likely to be found in the voluntary sector: in charities, in associations, in voluntary sector work.

Key findings
- profit-making establishments are more likely to be male-dominated than are non profit-making establishments
- women are likely to be found in the non profit-making areas of the economy
- ownership, profit-making and gender composition seem in fact to be functions of industry sector, and this emerges clearly throughout the survey as the defining issue by which all other variables can be understood.

Attributes of the jobs done by women and men

Given that women and men are largely segregated in different areas of the economy, and in different types of jobs, what particular characteristics do their jobs display? Do 'women's jobs' – concentrated at the bottom of occupational hierarchies, often defined as 'unskilled', and with generally poor access to vocational and on-the-job training – actually emerge as repetitious and poorly qualified?

Key Findings
- Most establishments are involved in activities which are relatively complex for the workforce to perform, but there is a greater proportion of repetitive tasks in female-dominated than in other types of establishment. Similarly, there is a greater proportion of complex tasks in male-dominated than in other types of establishment.
- Capital-intensity of establishment is associated with gender composition, with male-dominated and mixed-sex workplaces much more likely to invest in new technologies than female-dominated establishments.
- Low-skilled work is much more likely to be a characteristic of female-dominated establishments than of other types of establishment. High qualification work is much more a feature of male-dominated establishments.
- In industrial and technical areas, male-dominated establishments are most likely to require high qualifications. In white-collar areas, high qualification work is more characteristic of mixed-sex environments.

Table 3.9 *Repetitiousness or complexity of tasks by gender composition of establishment*

repetitiousness/ complexity of tasks	gender composition of establishment			
	male-only	male-dominated	mixed	female-dominated
repetitive	11	12	12	15
medium	14	16	17	13
complex	76	72	72	72
total (n)	100 (1069)	100 (1374)	100 (1162)	100 (4653)

Table 3.9 shows the gender differentiation of repetitious, middle-range, and complex jobs. Overall, surprisingly few establishments reported that their jobs were repetitious and surprisingly many (73%) reported the presence of complex work, and this might be a function of managements' perspectives on the work in their workplaces. It is also possible that the survey overall is biased in favour of workplaces which have complex jobs – that those which practise direct participation have been particularly assiduous in responding to the survey and that by definition these are also the establishments which are most likely to have complex work. Nevertheless, the proportion of tasks which are repetitious is slightly greater in female-dominated establishments than in other types of workplace, and complex tasks make up a greater proportion of tasks done in male-only establishments than in other types of establishment. This suggests that task complexity is more a feature of construction and manufacturing workplaces, presumably where skilled craft work continues to be important, while repetitive work is more characteristic of services employment. It does not present a very optimistic picture of women's access to varied and, by implication, more interesting work. It is possible, of course, that this picture may be modified when direct participation is practised and training is offered in preparation for organisational change; we examine the evidence for this possibility in Chapter 5.

Capital intensive workplaces are also more likely to be male-dominated or mixed-sex than to be female-dominated. Non technology-intensive workplaces are most likely to be female-dominated. This may be partly a sector effect – capitalising firms being in manufacturing and in new areas of the economy which are male-dominated but which are seeking to automate the expensive labour component of production. They are also likely to be mixed-sex sectors which are investing heavily in new technologies (financial services, for example). Previous studies of automation in many industries have shown that this process is often applied to men's work, and that subsequently jobs are redefined as 'female' once they are simplified and automated (Cockburn, 1983, 1985; Game and Pringle, 1984; Mitter, 1991). Although the EPOC survey does not confirm this – both capital intensive and non capital-intensive firms reported the same extent of increase in female employees – the gender composition of the survey workplaces is clearly associated with important differences in their application of technology.

Table 3.10 *Technological intensity by gender composition of establishment*

technological intensity of establishment	gender composition of establishment				
	male-only	male-dominated	mixed	female-dominated	all establishments
technology intense	22	32.5	27	18	100 (1516)
medium	28	30	24	18	100 (975)
not technology intense	21	27	26	27	100 (2154)
average	23	29	26	23	100 (4645)

Qualification requirements of work are often strongly divided along gender lines, as women have historically had much poorer access to skilled occupations and to training opportunities than have their male counterparts. In Chapter 5, we will consider the extent to which direct participation may serve to equalise access to training, or indeed may actually require improved and more equal training for its successful conduct. Here, however, we consider the gender dimensions of the qualifications and skills requirements of the EPOC survey establishments *regardless* of whether they practice direct participation. Put simply, we want to ask the question: do women in the survey establishments have equitable access to jobs requiring high qualifications?

Table 3.11 *Qualification requirements by gender composition of establishments*

qualification requirements of establishment	gender composition of establishment				
	male-only	male-dominated	mixed	female-dominated	all establishments
low qualification	20	24	24	33	100 (1006)
middle qualification	22	31	23	24	100 (1253)
high qualification	23	33	27	18	100 (2278)
average	22	30	25	23	100 (4537)

When we examine the presence of qualifications or skills by gender we find that low qualification work is much more likely to be found in female-dominated workplaces than in other types of workplaces. Equally, high qualification work is most found in male-dominated and mixed-sex workplaces (though there is a weak statistical correlation). This is not surprising – women have historically not enjoyed equal access to skilled work nor, particularly, to skilled status. In some industries – for example, printing – they have been actively excluded from these by their male counterparts (see Cockburn, 1983; Wajcman, 1991). The figures shown in Table 3.11 in part reveal a 'real' difference in levels of qualification between women and men. However, as important as this real difference is the ideological difference which has meant that significant areas of women's work have been socially defined as 'unskilled' simply by virtue of the sex of those who perform it (Phillips and Taylor, 1980). We cannot separate the real and the ideological components of 'skill' from one another in this survey data, but we can recognise the effects that this distinction may have.

If we examine the sectoral distribution of qualified work for women and men, this point becomes clear. Although in all sectors in the EPOC survey, the great majority of establishments reported having highly qualified work (see Appendix Table 3A5), in industries which have historically relied upon skilled male labour, highly qualified work continues to be disproportionately a province of men's workplaces. Table 3.12 shows that in the industrial and in the construction sectors, broadly defined, the majority of establishments with highly qualified work are either male-only or male-dominated. This of course reflects both the fact that all establishments in these sectors, regardless of qualification requirement, tend to be male-dominated or exclusively male, and the fact that qualified work in these sectors is much more a characteristic of men's than of women's jobs. In those sectors where women are present in greater proportions – the services industries and particularly establishments in the public sector – there are also more establishments with mixed-sex workforces which also have high qualification requirements. More than this, in the public sector, the majority of high qualification establishments are female-dominated. Just as with the construction and industrial sectors, this reflects partly the greater presence of women overall in these sectors, but also the fact that these sectors seem much more likely to give their women workers access to what high qualification work they do require.

The picture in Table 3.12 and Figure 3.5 is borne out by Table 3.13 and Figure 3.6. In establishments dominated by what might be called 'masculine', industrial occupations (i.e. skilled or semiskilled manual work in production, transport, and technical areas), it is the male-dominated establishments which report the greatest incidence of high qualification work. In white-collar and professional areas, the distribution of high qualification work is much more equitable between the sexes; mixed-sex workplaces report the greatest incidence of high qualification work. This reflects a greater presence of women in these areas of work but also much greater access by women to high qualification work, for example, in jobs as doctors, nurses, teachers, managers and administrators. We can also speculate that this data incorporates (but conceals) a difference in type of high qualification between the sexes. It is probable that the qualifications involved in the performance of highly qualified work in manual occupations are skills acquired through training and apprenticeships, whereas in white-collar areas they are more likely to be educational qualifications acquired through schooling and higher education. This pattern suggests that conventional gender inequalities in access to skill and to qualified work are being most significantly broken down in the white-collar occupations and industries, and that gender inequalities remain most firmly in place in the industrial and blue-collar areas of the economy[4].

Table 3.12 *Gender composition of establishments with work requiring high qualifications by industry sector of establishment (as percentages of all establishments in each sector)*

establishments in which work requires high qualification	\multicolumn{5}{c}{gender composition of establishment}
	male-only	male-dominated	mixed	female-dominated	all establishments (n)
industry	34	46	16	4	100 (745)
construction	73	21	3	3	100 (172)
trade	10	31	37	22	100 (366)
private services	15	32	40	12	100 (361)
public sector	6	23	33	37	100 (634)

---

[4] However, we found that establishments requiring low qualifications are no more likely to increase their female workforces than establishments requiring high qualifications (Table 3A6 in the Appendix).

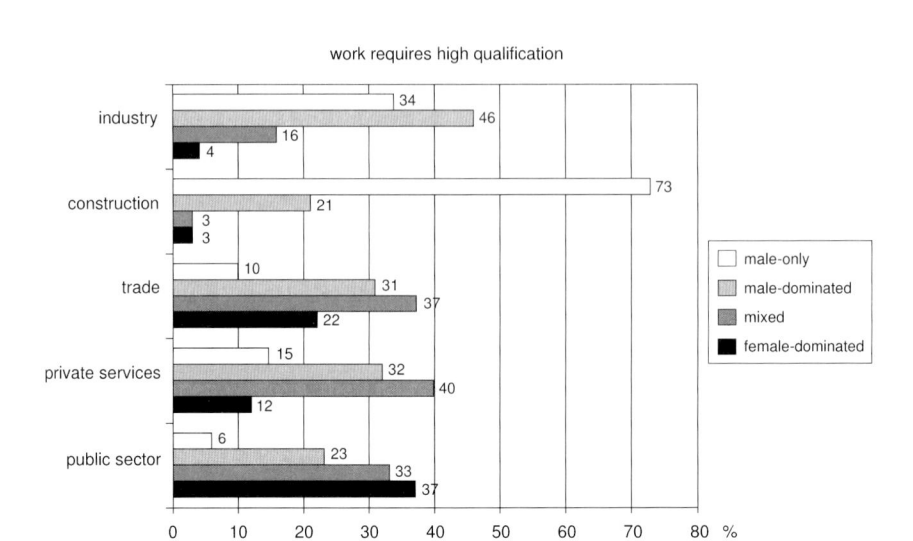

Figure 3.5 *The sectoral and gender distribution of high qualification work*

work requires high qualification

- industry: male-only 34, male-dominated 46, mixed 16, female-dominated 4
- construction: male-only 73, male-dominated 21, mixed 3, female-dominated 3
- trade: male-only 10, male-dominated 31, mixed 37, female-dominated 22
- private services: male-only 15, male-dominated 32, mixed 40, female-dominated 12
- public sector: male-only 6, male-dominated 23, mixed 33, female-dominated 37

Table 3.13 *Gender composition of establishments requiring high qualifications by dominant occupation of establishment (as percentage of all establishments in each occupational group)*

	\multicolumn{5}{c}{gender composition of establishment}
dominant occupation of establishments in which work requires high qualifications	male-only	male-dominated	mixed	female-dominated	all establishments (n)
production/transport	38	41	16	5	100 (858)
commercial/personal services	6	32	37	25	100 (383)
medical/education/ administration	3	12	45	40	100 (539)
repair/technical	36	55	7	1	100 (243)
average	23	33	27	17	100 (2023)

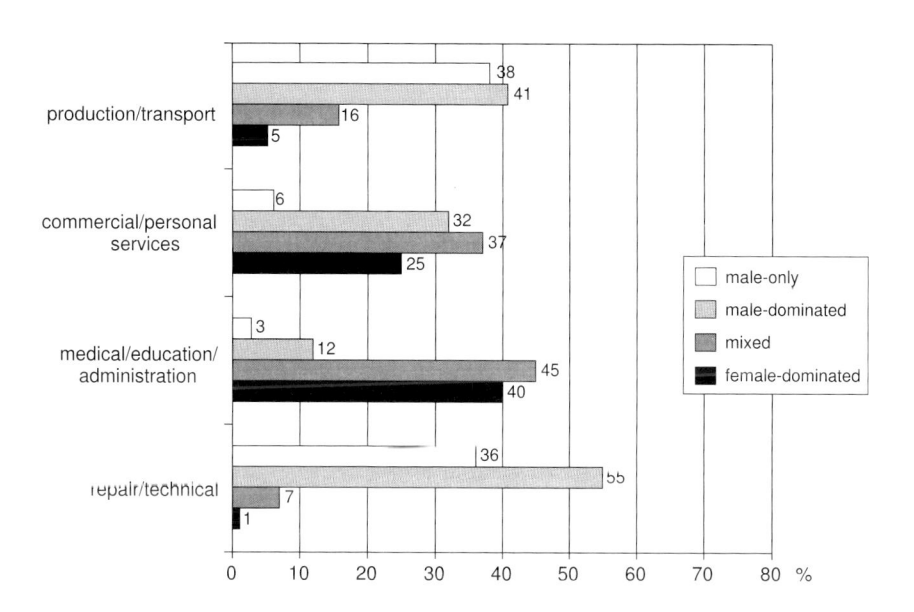

Figure 3.6 *The occupational and gender distribution of high qualification work*

	male-only	male-dominated	mixed	female-dominated
production/transport	38	16	41	5
commercial/personal services	6	32	37	25
medical/education/administration	3	12	45	40
repair/technical	36	55	7	1

Summary and conclusions

This initial overview of the gender structures of the EPOC workplaces confirms several widely understood aspects of women's work. It confirms our knowledge that women are segregated in a relatively narrow range of industry sectors and in a few occupational groups, and that there are significant areas of the economy where women are not found at all. It also strongly confirms the argument that developments in 'atypical employment' (the growth of part-time work, temporary work, subcontracting and other forms of non full-time, non lifetime employment) are firmly gendered. Part-time employment contracts are growing particularly rapidly in areas where women work, whilst temporary contracts and subcontracts are used more in areas where men work.

A critical point to emerge from the analysis thus far is that when we examine the characteristics of work and employment in the establishments surveyed, the key factor shaping the presence and position of women is industry sector. Women's participation within companies of different sizes, types of ownership and orientation to profit-making seems to be associated, not with these issues per se, but with the fact that they are themselves products of industry sector. Thus, for example, women's presence in private, non profit-making companies is likely in fact to be related to the fact that these companies are in sectors in which women are strongly represented. Similarly, when we look at company size, we can conclude that women's relative absence from large companies and their relative importance in smaller ones arises from the fact that large companies are usually in the extraction, manufacturing and construction industries. By contrast, although small companies do exist in all these sectors, they are more characteristic of the services sectors in which women are predominant – personal services like hairdressing; commercial services like hotel/catering and retailing; and increasingly (though our survey does not cover this issue), some emerging information-based services like marketing, advertising and information processing.

Although the evidence from this survey is not statistically very robust, it does also confirm existing understandings of the nature of women's and men's jobs. Repetitive and routine work seems to be more associated with female-dominated employment, and firms which make strong use of female labour seem to be less likely to make capital investments, perhaps because they have less need to than those which employ relatively expensive male labour. Finally, we are not surprised to find that women's work is likely to be lower skilled and less qualified than men's work. This is a complex issue, however, which has generated heated debate among analysts in the past. First, a distinction needs to be made between the skills inherent in the job and the skills of the job holder, and secondly, as we have already noted, it is critical to distinguish between the technical and the ideological aspects of skills before we can judge whether a person's work requires real competences or whether it has simply come to be labelled as skilled or unskilled through historical processes of collective bargaining and exclusionary practice.

These findings, of course, have important implications for women's access to direct participation and their ability to benefit from processes of direct participation. Are women located in sectors and jobs in which direct participation is practised? What implications does this have for their working lives? Does direct participation alter their conditions of work, their access to skills and training, and indeed their very employability? We examine these issues more closely in the rest of this report. First, we set the scene by discussing the gender patterns in direct participation – women's and men's access to it – uncovered in the EPOC survey.

References

Beatson, M., *Labour Market Flexibility*, Research Series No 48, Sheffield, Employment Department, 1995.

BIPE Conseil, *The effects on employment of the liberalisation process in the telecommunications sector*, Report to the Commission of the European Communities, 1996.

Cockburn, C., *Brothers: Male Dominance and Technological Change*, London, Pluto, 1983.

Cockburn, C., *Machinery of Dominance: Men, Women and Technical Know-How*, London, Pluto, 1985.

Cockburn, C., *In the Way of Women*, London, Macmillan, 1991.

Crompton, R. and Sanderson, K. *Gendered Jobs and Social Change*, London, Unwin Hyman, 1990.

European Commission, *Bulletin on Women and Employment in the EU*, No 9, Luxembourg, Office for Official Publications of the European Communities, October, 1996.

European Parliament, *Report on a Reduction in Working Hours*, Brussels, European Parliament Committee on Social Affairs and Employment, 1996.

Freeman, C. and Soete, L., *Work for All or Mass Unemployment: Computerised Technical Change into the 21st Century*, London, Pinter, 1994.

Game, A. and Pringle, R., *Gender at Work*, London, Pluto, 1984.

Goldmann, M., 'Industrial rationalisation as gender politics', *International Journal of Political Economy* 25, 4, 1995, pp. 65-90.

Goldmann, M., Kutzner, E., Riezler, M. and Aumann, K., *Perspektiven von Frauenarbeit bei neuen Produktions- und Managementkonzepten*, Dortmund, Sozialforschungsstelle, 1994.

Gratton, L., 'Competing through people', *Financial Times Mastering Management*, No 5, October, 1997.

Gunnarsson, E., 'Women and men – different rationalities?' in Gunnarsson, E. and Trojer, L. (eds), *Feminist Voices on Gender, Technology and Ethics,* Luleå, University of Technology Centre for Women's Studies, 1994.

Hakim, C., *Occupational Segregation*, Research Paper No 9, London, Department of Employment, 1979.

Harding, S., *The Science Question in Feminism*, Milton Keynes, Open University Press, 1986.

Hirdmann, Y., 'Genussystemet – reflexioner kring kvinnors sociala underordning', *Kvinnovetenskaplig Tidskrift* No 3, 1988.

Landes, D., *The Unbound Prometheus,* Cambridge, University Press, 1969.

Lay, G., *Neue Produktionskonzepte und Beschäftigung*, Karlsruhe, Fraunhofer ISI, 1997.

Marin, B., 'Flexible work sharing: the political economy of a reduction and reorganisation of working time'. Paper presented to European Commission seminar, *Working Time, Work Organization and Employment*, Brussels, September, 1996.

Meulders, D. and Plasman, R., 'Working time: new issues, new norms, new measures'. Paper presented to European Commission seminar, *Working Time, Work Organization and Employment*, Brussels, September, 1996.

Mitter, S., 'Computer-aided manufacturing and women's employment: a global critique of post-Fordism', in I. V. Eriksson, B. Kitchenham and K. Tijdens (eds), *Women, Work and Computerization: Understanding and Overcoming Bias in Work and Education*, Amsterdam, North-Holland, 1991.

Moldaschl, M., 'Frauenarbeit als Bastion des Taylorismus – keine Chancen für Qualifizierungsoffensiven in der Montage?', Munich, Institute for Social Research, 1992.

Neathey, F. and Hurstfield, J., 'Flexibility in Practice: Women's Employment and Pay in Retail and Finance', *Research Discussion Series* No 16, London, Industrial Relations Services, 1995.

Phillips, A. and Taylor, B., 'Sex and skill: notes towards feminist economics', *Feminist Review,* No 6, 1980, pp. 79-88.

Poynton, C., 'Naming women's workplace skills: linguistics and power', in Probert, B. and Wilson, B. (eds), *Pink Collar Blues: Work, Gender and Technology*, Melbourne, University Press, 1993.

Rubery, J., Smith, M. and Fagan, C., *Changing Patterns of Work and Working-Time in the European Union and the Impact on Gender Divisions*, Brussels, European Commission Equal Opportunities Unit, 1995.

Seitz, D., 'Gruppenarbeit in der Produktion. Ein Beitrag zur Systematisierung von Entwicklungsstand und Perspektiven', in Binkelmann, P., Braczyk, H-J., and Seltz, R. (eds), *Entwicklung der Gruppenarbeit in Deutschland*, Frankfurt-am-Main, 1993.

Shapiro, G. and Austin, S., *Equality Driven Total Quality*, University of Brighton Business School Occasional Paper Series No 3, 1996.

Sundin, E., 'The social construction of gender and technology – a process with no definitive answer', *European Journal of Women's Studies,* Vol 2, Issue 3, 1995, pp. 335-353.

Wajcman, J., *Feminism Confronts Technology*, Philadelphia, Penn State Press, 1991.

Webster, J., *Office Automation: the Labour Process and Women's Work in Britain,* Hemel Hempstead, Harvester Wheatsheaf, 1990.

West, J. (ed), *Work, Women and the Labour Market*, London, Routledge, 1982.

Woodfield, R., *'An ethnographic exploration of some factors which mediate the relationship between gender and skill in a software R&D unit'*, University of Sussex, DPhil thesis, 1994.

Chapter 4 Direct Participation and Gender

In Chapter 3, we saw how occupational segregation between women and men continues to operate in European workplaces, and how this sexual division of labour implies a series of other characteristics of establishments in which women work and in which men work. Women are employed in significant proportions in public services such as education, health and public administration, and in private services such as hotels/catering and culture/recreation. Their work is most likely to involve selling, providing personal services, catering, or providing health, education or social services. In those establishments in which large proportions of women are employed, their work is most likely to be repetitive and labour-intensive, requiring only low qualifications. Importantly, there are strong tendencies for their work to be 'casualised', through the increasing application of part-time employment contracts (which have historically been an important form of employment for women in many countries, particularly because they allow women to combine domestic responsibilities with paid employment). But not all the women in the EPOC survey were confined to only a few sectors and occupations; indeed, employment conditions vary not only between women and men but also between different groups of women.

In this context, the question arises of whether direct participation is relevant to women at all, and whether it is relevant to different women to the same extent. In the scientific literature, direct participation is an innovation which is usually linked to manufacturing, and even then only to certain types of manufacturing companies – namely, those which are seeking to develop new production systems which allow them to improve their ability to meet customer demand in the context of an increasingly competitive global market (Piore and Sabel, 1984; Kern and Schumann, 1984). The policy debate and scientific focus has, as the EPOC Research Group has noted, been particularly preoccupied with developments in one area of manufacturing – the automotive sector. The development and implementation of direct participation – in such forms as groupwork, teamworking, U-shaped assembly lines, cellular manufacturing, multiskilling, and functional flexibility – has been widely examined in these settings (Badham and Matthews, 1989; Dawson, 1994; Storey, 1994). To what extent can women, concentrated in service industries and in low-paid occupations in the lower echelons of organisations; often employed for their interpersonal skills but without skills or access to training; and often in routine and repetitive functions which are expressly designed to be so, gain access to direct participation and related initiatives? And if they do work in areas where direct participation is practised, what are the implications for equal opportunities between women and men? Does direct participation, and related initiatives which may be introduced alongside it carry advantages for women? Do these innovations – in promoting teams with configured competences, in requiring skills and the exercise of knowledge, in undermining conventional lines of demarcation which are often gendered as well as being skill-based, and in flattening hierarchies – help to overturn the sexual division of labour?

These are general questions which highlight the urgency of the task of considering the equal opportunities issues arising from direct participation. This chapter now analyses in more detail the role of gender relations in direct participation. The analysis focuses on the key components of sex segregation, such as sectoral and occupational segregation. For, although our understanding of organisational change has been significantly advanced by recent scientific studies, including the EPOC survey, as we have already noted, there is still a dearth of research, particularly quantitative and comparative research, into direct participation in the context of women's employment. However, the EPOC survey itself was not primarily designed for this purpose, and did not set out to confront particular hypotheses about the equal opportunities dimensions of direct participation. For this reason, the data derived from it is most usefully regarded as a heuristic instrument which reveals relationships between aspects of direct participation and the employment of women in the survey workplaces. From this evidence, we can only infer that particular gender divisions of labour determine the implementation of particular patterns of direct participation in the survey workplaces. Nevertheless, this in itself is of considerable value: it contributes to a better understanding of the gender dimensions of organisational change and in particular it supplies some quantitative information where none existed – especially on questions of men's and women's access to direct participation in its different forms, and on the effects of direct participation on equal opportunities.

The gender dimensions of direct participation

The results of the EPOC survey provide us with some useful indicators of the relationship between the practice of direct participation and the employment of women. First, the overall survey report (EFILWC, 1997) and the report on *Direct Participation in the Social Public Services* (Hegewisch et al, 1998) both indicate that direct participation is indeed relevant to women. They show that direct participation is strongly practised in sectors such as banking and insurance, professional services, public administration, health and social welfare. Indeed, all these economic sectors have high rates of direct participation *relative to their share of the economy as a whole* (see EFILWC, pp. 31-32 and Table 3.1). Banking and insurance, public administration, and health and social welfare are sectors in which there are significant numbers of women, so by implication we can expect to find women involved in direct participation. On the other hand, the hotels and catering, and culture, recreation and leisure sectors do not demonstrate high shares of direct participation relative to their total share of the economy, and these too are strong areas of 'women's work'. Nevertheless, it would seem that there is at least some potential for women to engage in direct participation in some of the sectors within which they are strongly represented. What does closer examination of the EPOC survey data tell us about this?

In Chapter 3, we examined the gender divisions of labour in the survey workplaces and the conditions of work associated with particular gender compositions of establishment. We saw that men and women are segregated in sectoral and in occupational terms, and that they also have different working conditions and employment contracts. The EPOC Research Group report shows that direct participation is also uneven: it is particularly prevalent in certain sectors and almost absent from others. We would therefore expect that women and men might have differential access to the practice of direct participation. In the remainder of this report, we are concerned with two sets of relationships between the practice of direct participation and gender. Our first concern, in this chapter, is with the gender composition of workplaces practising direct participation, and with the nature of the direct participation which is practised. Underlying this concern is the question of whether women and men have equality of access to direct participation. We can hypothesise, on the basis of existing studies of organisational change, that men and women do not have equality of access to direct participation, and that the extent and types of direct participation in which they are involved are differentiated. Our second concern, addressed in this and subsequent chapters, is with the reverse aspect of the relationship between direct participation and gender, the extent to which direct participation is associated with gender equity – in terms of access to occupations, training, and skills, and patterns of working time in practising workplaces. Given the widespread empirical evidence here and elsewhere of the powerful and enduring effect of structural workplace conditions on gender divisions of labour, we do not expect direct participation to have a major impact on gender relations and gender inequalities in workplaces. Moreover, the primary objective of establishments when they introduce direct participation is very unlikely to be to reduce gender inequality in their workforces. Any association between direct participation and increased gender equity will therefore be a by-product of introducing direct participation rather than a central aspect of it. Nevertheless, our second hypothesis is that direct participation is associated with greater gender equity than is the lack of direct participation.

Key findings
- Direct participation is practised by more than four-fifths of establishments, regardless of gender structure.
- Taking gender structure into account, mixed-sex establishments are the most likely to practise at least one form of direct participation.
- Services sectors which are key employers of women are important practitioners of direct participation.

Table 4.1 *Gender composition of establishments which practise direct participation*

direct participation	male-only	male-dominated	mixed	female-dominated	average
establishment does not practise	24	18	14	20	19
establishment practises	76	82	86	80	81
total	100	100	100	100	100
(n)	(1206)	(1565)	(1319)	(1186)	(5279)

Direct Participation and Gender

We start by looking at whether the practice of direct participation is related to the gender composition of the establishment. Is there, for example, a tendency for workplaces with different gender compositions to vary in their practice of direct participation?

Table 4.1 shows the four types of establishment by gender composition, and reports the proportions of each type practising and not practising direct participation. Overall, by far the majority of establishments practise direct participation – over 80% on average. The establishments most likely to report practising direct participation are mixed-sex establishments, and those most likely to report not doing so are male-only establishments. However, there is little substantial difference between the proportions of establishments practising direct participation across the gender groups – all types report practising it in more than three-quarters of cases.

In Figure 4.1, we invert the variables and consider the gender distribution within the two categories of establishments practising and not practising direct participation. This allows us to compare the gender composition of the two types of establishment, and, within the user group, to see which type of establishment is the most represented.

Figure 4.1 *Gender composition of establishments which practise/do not practise direct participation*

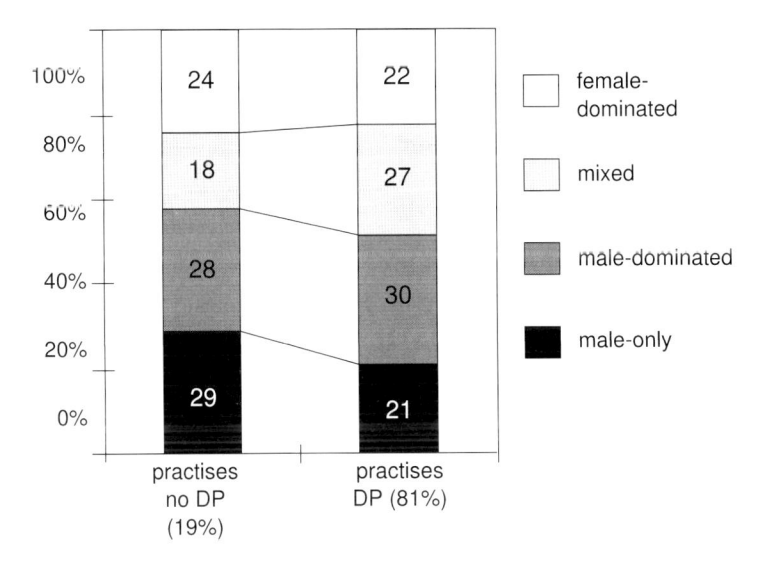

	practises no DP (19%)	practises DP (81%)
female-dominated	24	22
mixed	18	27
male-dominated	28	30
male-only	29	21

Table 4.2 Gender composition and country distribution of practitioner and non-practitioner establishments

country	establishment practising at least one form of DP					establishments not practising DP				
	male-only	male-dominated	mixed	female-dominated	total (n)	male-only	male-dominated	mixed	female-dominated	total (n)
DK	13	32	29	26	100 (551)	29	36	15	20	100 (100)
FR	23	25	22	28	100 (492)	38	18	18	25	100 (60)
GE	19	30	28	23	100 (616)	25	27	23	25	100 (138)
IR	20	25	29	25	100 (295)	40	24	16	20	100 (63)
IT	19	44	25	12	100 (362)	18	44	31	7	100 (90)
NL	30	39	23	8	100 (420)	43	23	17	17	100 (47)
PO	26	31	22	22	100 (167)	34	39	16	12	100 (95)
SP	13	37	28	22	100 (271)	24	37	21	18	100 (127)
SW	14	35	26	24	100 (644)	29	36	14	22	100 (59)
UK	15	32	30	22	100 (601)	33	23	22	22	100 (139)
average	19	33	27	22	100 (4379)	30	31	20	19	100 (918)

Direct Participation and Gender

From Figure 4.1, we can see that 30% of practitioner establishments are male-dominated, and 27% are mixed-sex. In the non-user group, the majority (29%) are male-only establishments, and only 18% are mixed. Mixed-sex establishments therefore make up a substantial proportion of the user group, while male-only establishments make up the greatest proportion of non-users; this confirms the results in Table 4.1. However, this data does not tell us which employees are covered by direct participation. It only shows that the largest occupational group within the establishments which are the most important practitioners of direct participation is a male-dominated or a mixed-sex occupational group. We still have to pursue the question of who is involved in direct participation and, since we are interested in equal access, whether women are included in the groups covered by direct participation. In order to answer this question, we have to develop measures which are tailored to showing women's representation within these groups, and this we do later in this chapter.

Table 4.2 shows the gender composition of practising and non-practising establishments in each country in the survey. It is clear from this that overall, more establishments practise direct participation than do not. This, then, confirms the figures shown in Table 4.1.

Comparing the gender composition of user and non-user establishments, male-only establishments are the main exceptions to this pattern. In most countries, mixed-sex and female-dominated workplaces are, like male-dominated ones, more likely to practise direct participation than not to do so. Exceptions are in Italy, Germany and the Netherlands where there are more non-practitioners than practitioners in the various types of establishment. Of particular interest to us here is the fact that, with the exception of Germany and the Netherlands, the proportion of female-dominated establishments which practise direct participation outweighs that of such establishments which do not practise it. Indeed, it is the male-only establishments which report the most significant levels of non-use, and this suggests that it is men in particular workplace settings (probably in sex-segregated industries like construction and extraction), rather than women, who are most excluded from direct participation. Table 3.1 in the previous chapter showed the gender composition of establishments by country and showed that on the whole, the gender composition of the survey establishments reflected the labour market participation rates of women in the different countries of Europe. The hypothesis that women's access to direct participation is stronger in countries in which their general labour market participation rates are highest and industrial democracy most strongly

Table 4.3 Gender composition and industry sector of establishments practising and not practising direct participation

	establishments practising DP					establishments not practising DP				
sector	male-only	male-dominated	mixed	female-dominated	all establish-ments	male-only	male-dominated	mixed	female-dominated	all establish-ments
industry	29	42	20	9	100 (1536)	28	39	17	16	100 (409)
construction	77	18	2	3	100 (261)	67	26	3	4	100 (116)
trade	12	25	33	30	100 (878)	23	7	18	51	100 (179)
private services	14	29	38	19	100 (680)	26	24	30	20	100 (153)
public sector	7	20	30	43	100 (930)	13	28	23	36	100 (133)
average	21	30	27	22	100 (4285)	30	28	18	24	100 (990)

developed (i.e. in the northern European and Nordic countries) is partially borne out by these figures. With the exception of the Netherlands, female-dominated and mixed-sex establishments are best represented in the practitioner groups in the northern European countries.

We now test our second concern: whether the strong association between sector and gender composition is influenced by direct participation. In other words: does direct participation disrupt established sectoral gender divisions of labour? In order to examine this issue, in Table 4.3 we compare the industry sector and gender composition of practising and non-practising establishments. (Here, industry sector is aggregated in order to produce figures which are statistically workable.)

This table shows that in the industry and trade sectors, greater proportions of female-dominated workplaces do not practise direct participation than do, while the reverse is the case for male-dominated workplaces. If, however, we compare the figures in this table to the pattern shown in Figure 3.2 in the previous chapter, it emerges that direct participation is most practised in organisations which have gender compositions 'typical' of their industry sector – and thus runs along predictable sector/gender lines. From this, it is not surprising to see that, for example, the majority of construction workplaces practising direct participation are male-dominated, while the majority of public sector organisations practising direct participation are female-dominated. However, it is also clear that while in sectors such as trade, in excess of 45% of establishments are female-dominated, only 30% of workplaces practising direct participation are female-dominated. In other words, workplaces with women present in large numbers are well represented in this sector overall, but less well represented in direct participation within the sector. The same is true of the public sector, though the difference between representation in the sector and representation in direct participation in the sector is smaller. Although there are some minor differences between users of direct participation and non-users, it seems that direct participation does not undermine existing gender divisions of labour by sector[1].

Relatively small numbers of establishments practise no direct participation, but they have specific gender characteristics which are worth noting. In fact, there is a much greater proportion of non-practising trade sector organisations which

---

[1] The measurements of association shown in the Appendix support this view: the differences between the indices are only minor.

are female-dominated (51%) than there is of practising ones (30%). On the other hand, a smaller proportion of female-dominated public sector organisations do not practise direct participation than do. There is an important message about the overall nature of women's access to forms of industrial democracy in general here. A relatively high proportion of female-dominated trade establishments not practising direct participation is consistent with the relatively low incidence of trade unionism and of general employee involvement, and the simultaneously high incidence of women's employment in the sector, particularly in retailing. Similarly, the higher proportion of female-dominated public sector establishments practising direct participation is consistent with the overall nature of the sector and in particular its reliance on team-based work planning. This is explored in more detail in the accompanying volume on *Direct Employee Participation in the Public Services* (Hegewisch et al, 1998). Overall, therefore, in the public sector, female-dominated establishments' access to direct participation closely mirrors the labour market participation rate of women in this sector in general. In other sectors, however, particularly in trade, female-dominated workplaces are much less well represented in direct participation as they are in the sector in general. This in fact paradoxically suggests that women's access to direct participation in this sector may be poor – that is, they may be present but not represented. We return to this issue later in this chapter when we develop a measure to assess both their presence and their representation. For the moment, however, we investigate further the relationship between the sexual division of labour in general and the gender dimensions of access to direct participation by considering the predominant occupation and gender composition of establishments practising and not practising direct participation. According to our second hypothesis, the association between occupation and gender division of labour, or gender structure, should vary only slightly between users of direct participation and non-users. Again, we assume that access to direct participation will not be strictly equal between the sexes, but will reflect broader patterns of occupational segregation by sex.

Table 4.4 shows that across all occupational groups in the largest occupational groups of the firms, female-dominated workplaces form greater proportions of non-practitioners of direct participation than of practitioners; male-dominated workplaces, on the other hand, form greater proportions of practitioners than of non-practitioners. However, mixed-sex workplaces are also more represented in the practitioner category, across all sectors, so the issue of lack of direct participation is an issue of sexually segregated workplaces (female-dominated ones and also male-only ones). Some establishments in which certain

Direct Participation and Gender

Table 4.4 Largest occupational group and gender composition of establishments practising direct participation

occupational group	establishments practising DP					establishments not practising DP				
	male-only	male-dominated	mixed	female dominated	total (n)	male-only	male-dominated	mixed	female dominated	total (n)
production, transport, warehousing	33	38	19	9	100 (1859)	40	33	13	15	100 (556)
commercial, personal services	5	27	37	32	100 (786)	4	10	26	60	100 (125)
medical/social care, education, administration	2	11	40	47	100 (766)	10	4	35	51	100 (119)
repair, maintenance, technical	36	47	15	3	100 (349)	32	52	13	3	100 (63)
average	21	31	27	21	100 (3760)	30	27	18	25	100 (863)

73

occupations predominate merit particular comment. The discrepancy between practitioner and non-practitioner workplaces is particularly marked in commercial and personal services establishments: 32% of practitioners are female-dominated, but a full 60% of non-practitioners are female-dominated. Mixed-sex workplaces in this occupational group are much more equally distributed in the practitioner and non-practitioner groups, as are male-only workplaces (though the proportions here are small). These occupations are, of course, overwhelmingly female-dominated in general, as we saw in Chapter 3, and the evidence of Table 4.4 suggests that there is substantial inequity between representation in the occupation and representation in the practice of direct participation. This inequity is more marked than in any other occupational area; in the other occupational area of strong female representation – medical/social care, education and administration – the discrepancy between practitioners and non-practitioners in female-dominated workplaces is much narrower, though it still exists.

The main forms of direct participation

Direct participation in one form or another would seem to be practised widely in European workplaces, regardless of the gender composition of those workplaces. Contrary to what we would expect given the nature and conditions of employment for many women, they do not seem to be excluded from direct participation initiatives, and in some sectors they actually seem to fare better than their male counterparts in this respect.

But direct participation can take a number of forms, which have been differentiated in this survey, and we might expect to see gender differences in the practice of these different forms.

- **Individual consultation (IC)**
  'Face-to-face': covers consultation between individual employees and their immediate managers (for example, regular performance reviews, regular training, development reviews, '360 degree' appraisal processes).
  Arm's length: covers arrangements which allow individual employees to express their views indirectly to management (for example, suggestion schemes, attitude surveys, speak-up schemes with counsellors, or ombudsmen).

- **Group consultation (GC)**
  Temporary groups: covers groups of employees who come together for a special purpose and for a limited period of time (for example, project groups or task forces).
  Permanent groups: covers groups of employees which discuss various work-related topics on an ongoing basis, such as quality circles.
- **Individual delegation**
  Individual employees are granted extended rights and responsibilities to carry out their work without constant reference back to managers – sometimes known as 'job enrichment'.
- **Group delegation**
  Rights and responsibilities are granted to groups of employees to carry out their common tasks without constant reference back to managers – most often known as 'group work'.

On the whole, we would expect women and men to be differentially covered by different forms of direct participation. We have already noted that developments in new production systems such as groupwork, teamworking, and multiskilling could be expected to be more characteristic of men's jobs in manufacturing industry than women's jobs in services. This supposition has not been supported by the EPOC data, but different forms of direct participation might still be gender-differentiated. For example, we might expect that male-dominated workforces, with their greater levels of trade unionisation and organisation for collective bargaining, would be more likely to practise group-based forms of direct participation than their female counterparts. We might also expect women, particularly those working with other women in female-dominated establishments, to be more strongly involved in consultative rather than in delegative forms of direct participation, since their employment in low-grade functions in many organisations does not apparently favour the application of either job enrichment or group work, which involve the deployment of a variety of skills as well as judgement and discretion.

Let us firstly consider whether women and men are differently involved in different forms of direct participation. Table 4.5 shows establishments which reported practising any one of the six forms; establishments may therefore be represented in more than one cell.

Table 4.5 and Figure 4.2 show the different forms of direct participation by the gender composition of the establishments practising them. From Table 4.5, we can see that **mixed-sex** workplaces practise all forms of direct participation more than other types of workplace (in a total of 1,137 cases), and **male-dominated** workplaces are the second greatest users of all these forms of direct participation (in 1,291 cases in total). Male-only workplaces report the lowest use of almost all forms.

Table 4.5 *Gender composition of establishments practising different forms of direct participation (expressed as percentages of each gender type of establishment; n=100%)*

form of direct participation	male-only (n=914)	male-dominated (n=1291)	mixed (n=1137)	female-dominated (n=944)	average (n=4286)[2]
arm's length individual consultation	45	52	48	43	47
face-to-face individual consultation	36	42	52	45	44
temporary group consultation	39	42	41	36	40
permanent group consultation	33	39	42	38	38
individual delegation	60	66	72	66	66
group delegation	37	40	43	40	40

Female-dominated workplaces also report a high incidence of individual delegation (66% of establishments practise it, as in male-dominated establishments), and 45% of these establishments also practise face-to-face individual consultation. Meanwhile, Figure 4.2 shows clearly that individual delegation is the most important form of direct participation practised in all establishments but particularly in mixed-sex environments. Furthermore, female-dominated establishments are no less inclined than their male counterparts to practise delegative forms of participation, although establishments with a female presence (mixed and female-dominated) seem rather more inclined towards face-to-face consultation than their male counterparts. One possible explanation for this is that face-to-face consultation is particularly characteristic of the public sector (Hegewisch et al, 1998), and the public sector is an important employer of women. It may also reflect the increasing use of techniques such as performance reviews, appraisals and measures within the services sector, particularly in areas of the public sector where increasing financial strictures have led to an increased emphasis on

---

[2] Minor variations in the total number of cases are possible for every form of DP because of item non-response.

Direct Participation and Gender

accountability. By the same token, arm's length consultation, which according to Table 4.5 is more widely used in male-dominated settings, is more common in the private sector, and particularly in private sector blue-collar employment.

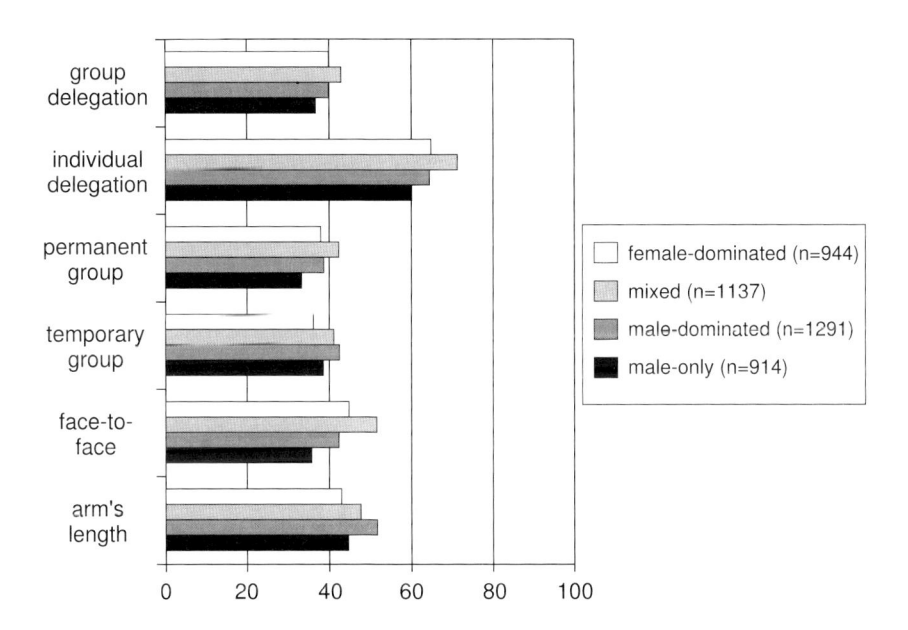

Figure 4.2 *Gender composition of establishments practising direct participation by form of direct participation practised*

Indeed, the results shown in Table 4.5 endorse the notion of a sectoral pattern of direct participation which the EPOC study has identified: male-only workplaces are often in sectors, such as the construction sector, which have been found to practise direct participation to a much lesser extent than other sectors, such as private services and public services. Male-dominated workplaces are in sectors such as manufacturing where all forms of direct participation are part and parcel of a wide repertoire of management practices, ranging from group technology to total quality management to quality circles to multiskilling. Mixed sex workplaces are more a feature of the services sector, both private and public, and, as we have seen, this sector has been identified as an important and growing user of direct participation (Hegewisch et al, 1998)[3].

---

[3] On the other hand, we found that there is virtually no form of direct participation which is more or less likely to be practised in any kind of establishment when we examined whether different forms of direct participation are systematically practised within establishments of different gender compositions (see Table 4A1 in the Appendix).

In addition, the relatively strong use of direct participation in mixed-sex workplaces might be understood by reference to a small number of previous studies of the gender relations of teamworking and similar innovations (Gunnarsson, 1994; Woodfield, 1994). These have suggested that teamworking arrangements may provide arenas in which women and men work more closely together and on the same level, and are therefore more likely to be gender-equitable than more traditional working arrangements. The results of the EPOC survey point in the same direction, but a much fuller understanding of the gender relations of teamworking, and of direct participation more broadly, is needed before this explanation can be confidently advanced. Moreover, the differences between different gender types of establishments in their practice of different forms of direct participation are so statistically small that we need to be cautious in drawing firm conclusions from them. Nevertheless, one way of addressing this issue through the EPOC survey is by examining the role of other factors in shaping gender patterns of direct participation, and in particular, the way in which different forms of direct participation may be used in combination with one another in establishments of different gender composition, and this we do next.

Key findings

- Mixed-sex workplaces report the greatest use of most forms of direct participation, with male-dominated workplaces being the next most frequent users.
- Male-only workplaces report the least use of direct participation in almost all its forms.

Examination of the number of forms of direct participation practised by establishments is one method by which we can explore the gender pattern of direct participation. We are interested in the mixed-sex workplaces: why do they seem to be more active practitioners than single-sex workplaces – the male-only group of establishments and the female-dominated group (which includes a tiny number of female-only workplaces too few to enumerate separately)? We would expect to find that the practice of multiple forms of direct participation is associated with integrated approaches by establishments to work organisation, such as Total Quality Management (EFILWC, 1997, p. 53), and it is possible that such integrated approaches to work organisation are associated with moves away from gender-typing in the workforce. In other words, we might expect establishments which are breaking down conventional lines of demarcation and divisions of labour to be less reliant on conventional patterns of occupational sex-typing which put men in certain areas of the workplace and women in other areas.

Table 4.6 *The incidence of multiple forms of direct participation by gender composition of establishments*

| | gender composition of establishment |||||
number of forms of direct participation practised	male-only	male-dominated	mixed	female-dominated	average (n)
none	24	18	14	20	19 (990)
one form	23	17	18	19	19 (1008)
two forms	21	22	18	20	20 (1067)
three forms	14	19	18	20	18 (934)
four forms	10	12	19	11	13 (688)
five forms	7	9	8	8	8 (423)
six forms	1	4	6	2	3 (166)
total	100	100	100	100	100 (5276)

Regardless of gender composition, most workplaces in the survey report practising two forms of direct participation. Very few – only 3% – practise all six forms. However, taking gender composition of workplace into account, the supposition that mixed-sex establishments might be more innovative in their approach to work organisation and practise more forms of direct participation is borne out by the figures in Table 4.6. 47% of male-only establishments practise none or only one form of direct participation, 58% of male-dominated establishments practise a maximum of three out of a possible six forms, while mixed-sex establishments are most likely to practise between one and four forms, and female-dominated establishments are most likely to practise between one and three forms. The establishments with well over the average incidence of practising all six forms are mixed-sex establishments, which supports our earlier expectation that integrated approaches to direct participation might be associated with more gender integration of workforces. It also supports the notion of 'Equality Driven Total Quality', which, as we saw earlier, emphasises the fact that organisational change must involve a coherent and integrated suite of practices if it is to be positive for gender equity. In terms of policy development, this is an encouraging indicator of moves in an equal opportunities direction. We must still treat it with caution, however, as the overall incidence of all six forms of direct participation is very small. Nevertheless, it is also worth noting that mixed-sex establishments are the least likely to report using no forms of direct participation at all. We have already noted earlier in this chapter that mixed-sex establishments are the most likely to practise direct participation, and Table 4.6 endorses our contention that a desegregated workplace is most closely associated with the implementation of participatory forms of organisational change. We cannot say which is the causal factor here, but we can suggest that perhaps these are workplaces which are innovatory across a number of dimensions, including their approach to the sexual division of labour and their implementation of organisational change.

The representation, coverage and intensity of direct participation

Women's representation and coverage in direct participation

We now wish to explore the question of gender equity in direct participation by examining the representation of women in the groups which are involved in consultation and delegation, as opposed to simply in the largest occupational groups of the establishments which practicse direct participation. We noted earlier that our results so far focus purely upon the practice of direct participation within the establishment and the gender composition of the largest occupational group of that establishment. However, this does not definitely show us which employees are involved in direct participation, and this issue is important from an equal opportunities viewpoint. If the mixed-sex aspect of workplaces which practise direct participation is meaningful, then we would expect the presence of women in the groups which are engaged in direct participation to be significant and not simply incidental. Moreover, previous research, including the EPOC survey, suggests that group forms of direct participation are particularly prevalent in male-dominated settings, so an analysis of the participation of women in these direct participation practices also helps to indicate the extent to which women are excluded from or included in the organisational life of these establishments.

Table 4.7 shows the representation of women in group consultation arrangements. The cells highlighted in bold type are those in which the gender composition of group consultation reflects the gender composition of the overall establishments. The cells above those in bold refer to the establishments where women are present in the workforce, but underrepresented in or excluded from group consultation. The cells below the bold areas refer to establishments where women are overrepresented in group consultation – that is, they are more

Direct Participation and Gender

prevalent in the group being consulted than they are in the establishment as a whole.

Table 4.7 *The gender composition of groups in establishments practising direct participation: group consultation*

	gender composition of establishment				
gender composition of group consultation	male-only	male-dominated	mixed	female-dominated	all establishments
male-only	**57**	28	10	5	100 (754)
male-dominated	7*	**63**	24	6	100 (814)
mixed sex	1*	14	**67**	18	100 (576)
female-dominated	5*	3	11	**82**	100 (401)
average	20 (506)	32 (806)	28 (704)	21 (520)	100 (2536)

* These cases are due to inconsistencies in the data

From the proportions shown in the table, it is possible to calculate that in 67% of establishments, women have access to group consultation arrangements commensurate with their presence in the workplace as a whole. In only 8% of establishments are women overrepresented. However, women are excluded from or underrepresented in group consultation arrangements in 27% of establishments which practise group consultation[4]. Under-representation takes place in 14% of all establishments, while women are excluded in 13% of the cases. In 43% (324 cases) of establishments – those with male-only workgroups (754 establishments) – women are totally excluded. In 31% of establishments (252 cases) – those which have male-dominated group consultation – women are underrepresented in proportion to their participation in the workforce of those establishments as a whole.

Table 4.8 shows the equivalent data for group delegation. In 68%[5] of establishments, women are involved in group delegation in line with their overall participation in the workforce. Total exclusion takes place in 12% of all establishments practising group delegation, while women are underrepresented in 13% of the cases. Only in 7% of establishments are they overrepresented in group delegation. However, they are totally excluded in 45% of workplaces, (those which have male-only group delegation), and in 31% of such workplaces they are underrepresented. Taken together, then, these two tables raise serious questions about the poor representation of women in group participation

[4] Total percentages are shown in Table 4A2 in the Appendix.
[5] Total percentages are shown in Table 4A3 in the Appendix.

processes; to a significant extent, they are present in the largest occupational groups in workplaces where group participation is practised, but are not involved in the groups themselves.

Table 4.8 *The gender composition of groups in establishments practising direct participation: group delegation*

gender composition of group delegation	gender composition of establishment			
	male-only	male-dominated	mixed	female-dominated	all establishments
male-only	**55**	29	11	5	100 (433)
male-dominated	7	**62**	22	8	100 (457)
mixed-sex	1	11	**76**	12	100 (355)
female-dominated	8	2	10	**81**	100 (248)
average	20 (295)	30 (453)	30 (442)	20 (303)	100 (1493)

Key findings

- 27% of establishments practising group consultation underrepresent or totally exclude their female employees from participation in these groups. (Under-representation takes place in 14% of all establishments while women are excluded in 13% of the cases.)
- 25% of establishments practising group delegation underrepresent or totally exclude their female employees from this participation. (Total exclusion takes place in 12% of all establishments practising group delegation, while women are underrepresented in 13% of the cases.)

The results in Tables 4.7 and 4.8 indicate that the representation of women in direct participation is an issue which merits further attention. It seems that in a large proportion of establishments, female employees are not covered by group consultation or delegation. It is therefore worth examining this issue in more detail, and in particular, comparing the coverage of women in direct participation with that of the workforce as a whole. For although we have seen that women are poorly covered in groups, we have not yet explored the overall dimensions of coverage and this is necessary in order to be able to draw reliable conclusions on the exclusion of women from group participation. We now present information on the wider coverage of group participation inside the EPOC establishments. This provides a more precise picture of the representation or exclusion of female workers from groups.

The coverage of direct participation refers to the proportion of the largest occupational group involved in direct participation. As the EPOC Research

Group report points out, an establishment may practise a particular form of direct participation, but this could only involve a small number of employees or it could embrace the total number. Equally, a respondent may have indicated that women are involved in direct participation, but, as we have already learned, this could either be a minority or the whole cohort of women in the establishment. Coverage of direct participation is particularly an issue, and most straightforward to assess, in relation to group forms of direct participation. It is much more feasible, and indeed much more instructive, to measure the proportion of the workforce in an establishment involved in the group than it is to measure the proportion involved in individual forms of participation which may in any case be open to all employees. However, in the case of group participation, the extent of coverage of the workforce gives a strong indication of the extent of commitment by the establishment to such a strategy. The wider the coverage, the more effective the practice is likely to be.

In order to assess the gender dimensions of group participation coverage, we start from the measures derived from Tables 4.7 and 4.8, measures of the representation of women in group participation in relation to their representation in the entire establishment. In combination with this measure, we use the measure of coverage of the total workforce in group participation. By combining the two, we have developed a set of indicators for:

- establishments with a low coverage of both their whole workforce and their female employees;
- establishments with a high coverage of their whole workforce but a low coverage of their female employees;
- establishments with a low coverage of their whole workforce but a high coverage of their female employees; and
- establishments with a high coverage of both their whole workforce and their female employees.

Table 4.9 *Coverage of female employees and of the workforce as a whole: group consultation*

establishments' coverage of **all** employees in the largest occupational group	establishments' coverage of **female** employees in the largest occupational group		
	Low (-49%)	High (50+%)	Total
Low (-49%)	36	20	56
High (50+%)	22	22	44
Total	58	42	100 (1768)

Table 4.9 shows that, taking into account the coverage of all employees as well as of female employees in group consultation, women are underrepresented in relation to employees as a whole in 22% of establishments; are overrepresented in 20% and are represented in line with overall employee representation in 58% of establishments[6]. Unlike Tables 4.7 and 4.8, this table does not, however, distinguish establishments in which women are totally excluded from consultation processes[7].

We would expect the representation of women and of employees in general to be differentiated by industry sector. We know that direct participation is variable by sector, and that so too is sexual segregation a function of sector. Table 4.10 shows the sectoral breakdown and gender dimensions of the coverage of group consultation.

Table 4.10 *Gender coverage of group consultation by sector*

sector	coverage of workforce low; coverage of women low	coverage of workforce high; coverage of women low	coverage of workforce low; coverage of women high	coverage of workforce high; coverage of women high	all establish-ments
industry	49	26	17	8	100 (545)
construction	79	12	7	2	100 (43)
trade	36	20	26	19	100 (424)
private services	29	20	18	33	100 (273)
public sector	21	24	20	35	100 (483)
average[8]	36 (635)	22 (398)	20 (352)	22 (383)	100 (1768)

Table 4.10 confirms that the gender dimensions of group consultation coverage are indeed differentiated by industry sector. Women are poorly represented in industrial and construction workplaces (although in the majority of both these types of workplace coverage is in general poor). They are well represented – indeed overrepresented – in 26% of establishments in the trade sector, and they are well but equitably represented in over one-third of firms in both the private services sector and in the public sector. On average, a greater proportion of workplaces underrepresent than overrepresent women (23% compared to 20%),

---

[6] Differences in the percentages presented in Table 4.7 are due to the grouping in Table 4.9 and the different non-response rates.
[7] Table 4A2 gives an overview of the gender coverage of direct participation differentiated by gender composition of the establishments.
[8] Differences between the averages and the figures in Table 4.9 are due to sectoral figures omitted from this Table.

Direct Participation and Gender

indicating that there remains room for improvement in the representation of female employees in group consultation. What, then, are the gender dynamics of group delegation?

Table 4.11 *Coverage of female employees and of the workforce as a whole: group delegation*

establishments' coverage of **all** employees in the largest occupational group	establishments' coverage of **female** employees in the largest occupational group		
	Low (–49%)	High (50+%)	Total
Low (-49%)	31	20	51
High (50+%)	25	24	49
Total	56	44	100 (1055)

Table 4.11 shows that for group delegation, female employees are underrepresented in a full quarter of establishments[9], are overrepresented in one-fifth of them, and are equitably represented in 55% of workplaces. We would expect the sectoral patterns of representation for group delegation to be similar to those for group consultation[10].

Table 4.12 *Gender coverage of group delegation by sector*

sector	coverage of workforce low; coverage of women low	coverage of workforce high; coverage of women low	coverage of workforce low; coverage of women high	coverage of workforce high; coverage of women high	all establishments
industry	41	32	20	7	100 (280)
construction	69	31	0	0	100 (13)
trade	39	12	21	29	100 (221)
private services	24	21	24	31	100 (167)
public sector	21	19	24	36	100 (288)
average[11]	32 (311)	22 (210)	22 (210)	25 (238)	100 (969)

Similarly, though the data here is less robust, Table 4.12 indicates that three sectors – industry, construction and trade – have low coverage of their

---
[9] Differences in the percentages presented in Table 4.7 are due to the grouping in Table 4.9 and the different non-response rates.
[10] Table 4A3 in the Appendix gives an overview of the gender coverage of direct participation differentiated by the gender composition of the establishments.
[11] Differences between the averages and the figures in the Table 4.11 are due to sectoral figures omitted from this Table.

workforces as a whole within group delegation arrangements, while two – private services and public services – have high coverage of their workforces as a whole. In the first instance, women are also weakly covered, and in the second, they are also strongly covered. This suggests (though we have to be cautious in interpreting this data) that group delegation is strongest in the services sector and that here women have as good quality access to it as do their male counterparts. On average in group delegation, women are underrepresented as often as they are overrepresented, so the problem of representation is not a problem of all forms of direct participation, or of all industry sectors.

The intensity of direct participation

We have seen that direct participation is reported in a relatively high number of establishments. However, the simple incidence of direct participation does not tell us anything about the quality of that participation. One way in which we can consider the quality, as opposed to simply the incidence of its practice, is to examine the number and range of issues upon which employees are consulted or have delegated decision-taking responsibilities. These issues may, for example, include work organisation, working time, health and safety, training and development, quality of product or service, customer relations, changes in technology, and changes in investment. In the survey report (EFILWC, 1997, p. 55) this is described as the 'scope' of direct participation, and workplaces are grouped into high, medium or low scope categories, depending on the number of forms and the range of issues combined. Though we refer instead to the 'intensity' of direct participation here, we continue to use the categories of high, medium and low intensity direct participation as our measures.

Table 4.13 *Intensity of direct participation by gender composition of establishment*

intensity of direct participation	male-only	male-dominated	mixed-sex	female-dominated	average
low	59	52	50	54	54
medium	35	40	40	38	39
high	6	7	10	8	8
total (n)	100 (914)	100 (1291)	100 (1137)	100 (944)	100 (4286)

Table 4.13 shows that on average, most establishments practise only low intensity – or we might say low quality – direct participation. Male-only establishments are most likely to report low intensity direct participation, and

Direct Participation and Gender

mixed-sex ones are least likely to do so. Indeed, mixed-sex workplaces also report the greatest proportion of high intensity practitioners. When we take the results of this table in conjunction with those in Table 4.7, we see that mixed-sex workplaces practise not only the most forms of direct participation, but they also practise the highest quality direct participation. However, we have to remember that the differences between the cells here are not major ones, and it therefore seems that the quality of direct participation is not associated with gender. There may, however, be a stronger association between individual forms of direct participation, their quality and gender. In particular, the presence of high intensity group delegation in establishments with significant proportions of women might indicate that the notion of Equality Driven Total Quality has been taken up and applied by some of the establishments in this survey. This issue is explored in Table 4.14.

Table 4.14 *Intensity of group delegation by gender composition of establishment*

intensity of group delegation	gender composition of establishment				
	male-only	male-dominated	mixed-sex	female-dominated	average
high	20	25	25	25	24
medium	47	31	34	42	40
low	32	44	40	33	35
total (n)	100 (338)	100 (516)	100 (490)	100 (378)	100 (1722)

Most establishments report medium intensity group delegation, and we find no difference between male-dominated and female-dominated establishments in their propensity to practise high quality group delegation. It would seem therefore that group delegation, where it is practised, is not noticeably part of a wider equal opportunities agenda in firms.

Table 4.15 reports only establishments using low intensity direct participative forms. Medium and high intensity forms are omitted because their combined incidences are too small to offer us conclusive results, but we can note that in each gender category their inclusion with each low intensity would constitute 100% of cases in that gender category. This table shows, overall, that consultative forms of direct participation are more likely to be low intensity than are delegative forms. It is clear, too, that low intensity direct participation is more likely to feature in male-only or male-dominated settings than in mixed or female-dominated ones, with the exception of temporary group consultation, which is especially likely to be low intensity in female-dominated establishments. The lower incidence of low intensity participation in settings where women are present in some numbers indicates that the number and range of issues upon which employees are consulted or invited to decide is much broader in settings where there are women (principally in services and the public sector) than where there are men. However, as we have already seen, this is not the same as saying that female employees themselves are included in such participation.

Table 4.15 *Establishments reporting low intensity of each form of direct participation by gender composition (expressed as percentages of each gender category)*

low intensity of different forms of direct participation	gender composition of establishment					all establishments practising this form
	male-only	male-dominated	mixed	female-dominated	total (n)	
arm's length individual consultation	59	56	55	53	56 (1132)	2025
face-to-face individual consultation	49	53	59	47	53 (991)	1877
individual delegation	41	34	31	37	35 (995)	2847
permanent group consultation	52	46	43	42	45 (743)	1640
temporary group consultation	50	56	51	63	55 (928)	1689
group delegation	32	44	30	33	35 (609)	1722

Key findings

- In those environments where the coverage of direct participation is wide, particularly in private and public services, women have equitable representation in direct participation groups.
- On balance, a greater proportion of workplaces underrepresent than overrepresent women, and this indicates that there remains room for improvement in the representation of female employees, particularly in the practice of group consultation.

- Mixed-sex establishments offer most forms of direct participation with the highest scope, and greater scope seems to be associated with progressively more sexually-mixed environments.

The organisational arrangements associated with direct participation

We have examined the patterns of direct participation in the context of the gender division of labour operating within the establishments in the survey, and we have established that direct participation is not strongly divided along gender lines. Though large proportions of women are excluded from group consultation and group delegation specifically, they seem to be better represented in all forms of direct participation when they work in mixed-sex environments. Services, and particularly private services, are strong practitioners of direct participation and they are also strong employers of women.

We now therefore have some quantitative understanding of the gender dynamics of direct participation. It would be interesting to supplement this with some **qualitative** analysis of these dynamics. What other initiatives do establishments introduce alongside direct participation when they introduce this in mixed or strongly female environments? We know that establishments which introduce direct participation generally introduce other initiatives alongside it, and the more forms of direct participation which are introduced, the more initiatives accompany it (EFILWC, 1997). Are these initiatives different when male and female-dominated workforces are involved? Do men benefit differentially from organisational measures which often involve knowledge utilisation and skills deployment (such as strategic alliances or back-to-core-business moves involving strong in-house R&D activity), because they have disproportionately high access to these types of work? Or are they more susceptible to simple rationalisation initiatives like employment reduction or management reduction?

Key findings
- Around one-third of establishments practising direct participation have introduced associated management initiatives.
- Male-dominated organisations show the greatest propensity to introduce various other management initiatives alongside direct participation.
- Working-time initiatives, particularly part-time working, are very likely to be used in female-dominated establishments practising all types of direct participation. The equal opportunities implications of this development are less potentially positive.

Table 4.16 *Management initiatives accompanying direct participation (DP) by gender composition of establishments*

Initiatives	male-only	male-dominated	mixed	female-dominated	all establish-ments practising DP	proportion of all DP practitioners
working time reduction	24	28	21	27	100 (474)	11
working time flexibility	17	30	27	27	100 (1385)	32
downsizing	24	29	26	20	100 (996)	23
outsourcing	30	33	20	17	100 (623)	15
back to core business	21	34	28	17	100 (601)	14
strategic alliances	16	44	23	16	100 (555)	13
product innovation	19	35	29	17	100 (1296)	30
new information technology	16	31	27	26	100 (1712)	40
automation	23	37	25	15	100 (898)	21
average	19	33	25	20	100	20

(Columns grouped under "gender composition of establishment": male-only, male-dominated, mixed, female-dominated.)

Table 4.16 shows that regardless of the gender composition of the establishment, the most widespread management initiative accompanying the implementation of direct participation is the introduction of new technology. Given the recent emphasis in academic and consultancy literature alike on the necessity to rethink organisational practices when implementing new technologies, it is possible that the survey workplaces have heeded this advice and adopted direct participation practices in order to smooth the implementation process and derive the greatest benefit from the application of new technologies.

Male-dominated establishments practising direct participation are slightly more likely than other establishments to introduce associated initiatives, though there is some variation between the forms of initiative introduced and the gender composition of establishment. Aside from the overall prevalence of male-dominated workplaces in the EPOC survey, there are some discernible gender patterns in the different initiatives which are introduced.

The application of various management initiatives is more strongly in evidence in male-dominated than in other workplaces. Specifically, downsizing, flattening of management structures, outsourcing and moves back to the core business have all been advocated as re-engineering techniques and have been most particularly implemented in large scale, high-complexity manufacturing industries, for example, in engineering and in the automotive industry. It is therefore not surprising to find that these techniques are characteristic of male-dominated workplaces, but it suggests that some of the accompanying initiatives to direct participation might have some negative consequences for the men who work in these establishments, particularly redundancies associated with downsizing and outsourcing of work.

On the other hand, for those whose jobs are not affected by downsizing, some of these initiatives are potentially very positive for the type of work they do and for their personal development prospects. We see in Table 4.16, too, that male-dominated workplaces are the most likely to venture into strategic alliances, to engage in product and process innovation, and to introduce greater involvement of lower-level employees. Strategic alliances, at least at the higher echelons of organisations, allow for collaboration in product development and potentially high knowledge-content work, which is more likely to be a feature of men's jobs than of women's. Process innovation is, of course, double-edged, signalling both improvements in employees' expertise but also job loss in the routine areas of organisations. All these initiatives are found more in male-dominated than in female-dominated establishments.

Meanwhile, female-dominated establishments report the greatest proportion of working-time flexibility initiatives (which is likely to indicate part-time and other forms of flexible employment contract). We have already discussed the increase of part-time work in female-dominated establishments in Chapter 3 (see Figure 3.3), and here we have an indication that this is the key innovation associated with the move to direct participation affecting such establishments. This is not as potentially promising for women – and therefore for equal opportunities – as are some of the other innovations which are applied in more strongly male settings. Part-time work is not particularly associated with full employee integration within the organisation, nor with access to training, exercise of on-the-job knowledge and expertise, and improvements in employee development and career prospects.

Is the association of part-time contracts with women's employment different when different types of direct participation are practised? We can assume that part-time working is common across all types of women's employment, but it may be particularly associated with particular types of direct participation, such as the consultative forms which do not rely so heavily upon the full-time presence of employees as delegative forms perhaps do. Table 4.17 shows the gender composition of those establishments which have increased their part-time contracts and the forms of direct participation which they practise.

Table 4.17 *Gender composition of and form of direct participation used in establishments which have increased part-time work (percentages of all establishments)*

type of direct participation	gender composition of establishment				
	male-only	male-dominated	mixed	female-dominated	all establish-ments (n)
arm's length individual consultation	7	15	36	51	26 (454)
face-to-face individual consultation	5	17	40	57	31 (493)
individual delegation	8	16	36	47	27 (646)
temporary group consultation	9	15	34	48	26 (357)
permanent group consultation	6	20	37	56	31 (416)
group delegation	8	17	40	52	30 (415)

This table shows the strength of the association between gender composition of establishment and the propensity to increase the use of part-time labour. Regardless of type of direct participation practised, mixed-sex and female-dominated establishments emerge as very strong part-time employers, together making up the vast majority of establishments increasing their part-time work, so increases in part-time employment do not seem to be associated with different forms of participation. In other words, the increase in part-time work is equally marked for all types of direct participation. This is clearly illustrated in Figure 4.3.

Direct Participation and Gender

Figure 4.3 *Gender composition of and form of direct participation used in establishments which have increased part-time work*

form	male-dominated	mixed	female-dominated
arm's length individual consultation	22	36	51
face-to-face individual consultation	22	40	57
individual delegation	24	36	47
temporary group consultation	24	34	48
permanent group consultation	26	37	56
group delegation	25	40	52

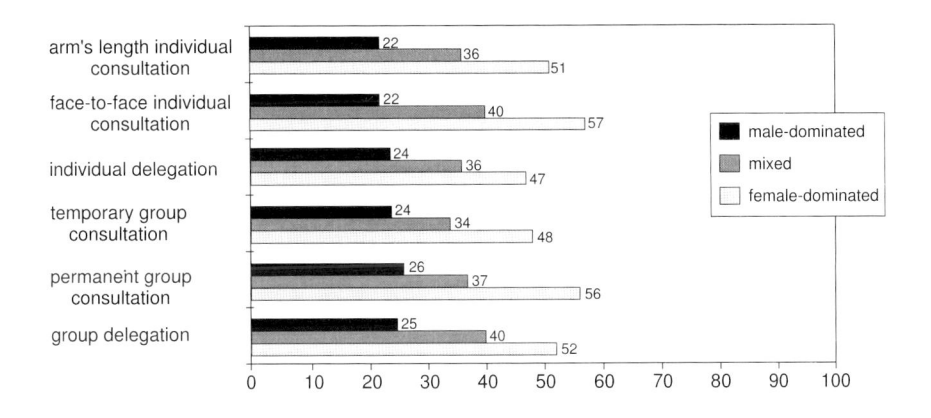

Table 4.18 *Gender composition of and form of direct participation used in establishments which have increased temporary work (percentages of all establishments)*

type of direct participation	male-only	male-dominated	mixed	female-dominated	all establishments (n)
arm's length individual consultation	32	28	25	28	28 (449)
face to face individual consultation	33	35	32	37	34 (491)
individual delegation	27	25	28	28	27 (585)
temporary group consultation	31	30	32	29	30 (410)
permanent group consultation	31	29	22	37	29 (365)
group delegation	31	30	30	34	31 (406)

In Table 4.18 and Figure 4.4 we see again the relationship between gender structure and employment contract. Here, increases in temporary working are shown to be most prevalent in organisations practising direct participation which are male-dominated, reflecting overall patterns of temporary employment shown in Chapter 3. Again, there is little difference between organisations practising different forms of direct participation, and indeed the number of cases overall is too small for any significant lessons to be drawn concerning the distribution of temporary contracts by type of direct participation practised. Figure 4.4 shows these results in bar chart form.

Figure 4.4 *Gender composition of and form of direct participation used in establishments which have increased temporary work*

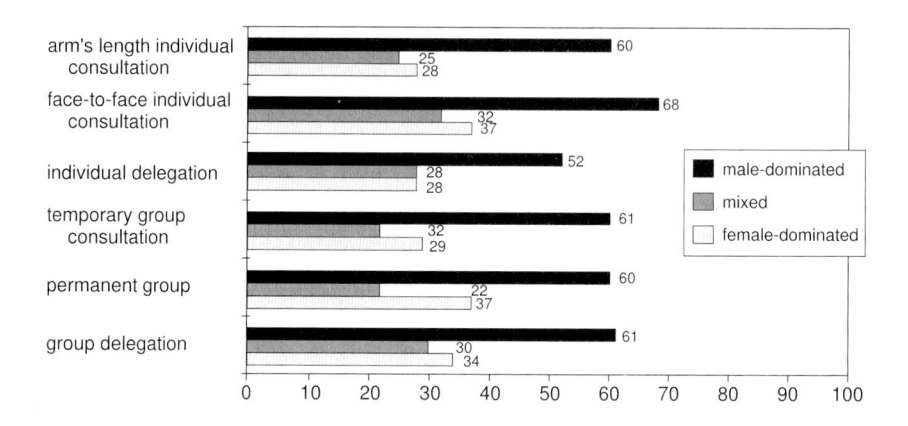

Form of direct participation	male-dominated	mixed	female-dominated
arm's length individual consultation	60	25	28
face-to-face individual consultation	68	32	37
individual delegation	52	28	28
temporary group consultation	61	32	29
permanent group	60	22	37
group delegation	61	30	34

Our final look at the gender dimensions of direct participation involves an examination of the qualification requirements of workplaces practising direct participation according to their gender composition (which we can compare to workplaces not practising direct participation). So far, it seems that direct participation is associated with different working conditions and with different management initiatives in organisations with different gender compositions. On the whole, male-dominated workplaces seem to be mainly located in the manufacturing sector; they seem to practise direct participation in the context of reduced employment security through downsizing; product and process innovation; and, for those employees still in employment, some promising opportunities for personal development through participation in strategic alliances. Mixed-sex and female-dominated workplaces practising direct participation are, by contrast, mainly in the services sector and within that, mainly in public services. Rather than downsizing and associated employment reductions, flexible working arrangements (specifically part-time work increases) are more likely to take place in female-dominated environments. What type of skills and qualifications, then, do these establishments require in their workforces?

Table 4.19 *Qualification requirements in establishments by the gender composition of the establishment*

qualification level required	male-only	male-dominated	mixed	female-dominated	total (n)
practitioners of direct participation:					
low level	20	23	25	31	100 (741)
high level	25	32	28	17	100 (1962)
non-practitioners of direct participation:					
low level	19	25	18	37	100 (265)
high level	21	39	20	20	100 (317)

Table 4.19 shows that qualification levels required of workforces are gender-differentiated both in establishments practising direct participation and in those not practising it. In workplaces practising direct participation, the highest proportion using only low level qualifications is among female-dominated organisations, while conversely the lowest proportion using high level qualifications is also among female-dominated organisations. Though the number of cases and therefore the reliability of the data is lower in workplaces which do not practise direct participation, the association between gender composition and qualification level is not much higher. Female-dominated workplaces dominate the group using low level qualifications and are most poorly represented among those using high level qualifications. These figures confirm the view that women's work is largely concentrated in the low-skill, low-grade areas of employment. The practice of direct participation seems to slightly lower the association between women's work and low level qualification requirements, but the number of cases involved here is so small that it is impossible to conclude confidently from them that female employees stand to gain opportunities for using higher qualifications or that direct participation serves to redress women's disadvantage in access to higher qualification jobs. We examine in more depth the effects of direct participation upon equal opportunities along a number of dimensions in the next chapter.

Summary and conclusions

Women's representation in practices of direct participation is surely an important indicator of the effectiveness of those practices, particularly in fulfilling an equal opportunities agenda. How well, then, are women represented? Could direct participation practices be used to enhance women's role in workplace reorganisation, and indeed to ensure that their needs and requirements are met in such processes?

When we examined the intensity of direct participation, we found that low intensity direct participation is more likely to feature in male-only or male-dominated settings than in mixed or female-dominated ones, with the exception of temporary group consultation, which is especially likely to be low intensity in female-dominated establishments. Although we have no information about access to high intensity direct participation by female employees as individuals, we can conclude that at establishment level, those with a high proportion of female workers practise direct participation at a very similar level of intensity to male-dominated establishments.

The EPOC survey shows that 86% of mixed sex establishments which responded to the survey practise direct participation. This makes these establishments the most assiduous practitioners of direct participation, and by implication, women within these establishments are involved in direct participation initiatives. We know, too, that direct participation seems to be most practised in establishments where the gender composition is 'typical' of the sector overall, so that, for example, in mixed-sex sectors it is mixed-sex establishments which most practise direct participation. Where women are employed in particular sectors, therefore, they are also involved in direct participation in establishments in those sectors which practise it. When occupational patterns of direct participation are considered in relation to gender, female-dominated and mixed-sex establishments in the different occupational categories still show high levels of direct participation, suggesting further that women are strong participants in these arrangements.

Mixed-sex workplaces are also important practitioners of all **forms** of direct participation, second only to male-dominated establishments. They are leading practitioners of face-to-face individual consultation, probably because this involves techniques which are widely used in the public sector where mixed-sex workforces are particularly dominant. They are also, importantly, leading practitioners of multiple (between four and six) forms of direct participation, and lead in the practice of high scope participation. Previous studies suggest that such arrangements are very positive for women and foster their advancement in organisations because they are often associated with teamworking and flatter hierarchies – environments in which it is suggested that women flourish. On the face of it, then, this would seem to indicate potentially positive developments in the direction of equity of access to direct participation.

However, changing the unit of analysis and looking at the gender composition of groups involved in group consultation and delegation specifically, we find that around one-quarter of establishments either exclude women from these groups altogether, or do not include them in proportion to their overall participation in the labour force. So despite the importance of mixed-sex workplaces as practitioners of direct participation, their female employees are not always properly or fully represented in that participation. Moreover, the qualification requirements in these settings, and in female-dominated settings, are generally low, particularly compared to male-dominated direct participation.

Under-representation of women in direct participation is particularly the case in male-dominated industrial sectors, where, in between one-quarter and one-third of organisations, women are underrepresented in direct participation. Given the tendency in these organisations for women to be employed in semiskilled or unskilled areas of production, it is possible that direct participation arrangements systematically exclude employees there in favour of employees in more skilled areas of work. Indeed, the fact that male-dominated establishments are the most active in introducing other initiatives alongside direct participation indicates that in these organisations, managements have introduced entire suites of changes and have strongly involved their male skilled manual employees, whilst leaving other employees completely untouched by their initiatives. Of course, this is not to say that these initiatives are necessarily positive for employees, as we have seen earlier in the chapter.

Overall, it would seem that, although mixed-sex environments are the most active users of direct participation along a number of dimensions, the women within them and in female-dominated environments have patchier access to forms of direct participation which require fewer skills than do their male counterparts. This does not indicate that direct participation has been implemented in order to promote women's needs and requirements or to enhance equal opportunities objectives at work, at least in any way which could signal a long-term and sustainable improvement in the sexual segregation of labour.

References

Badham, R. and Matthews, J., 'The new production systems debate', *Labour and Industry*, 2, 2, 1989, pp. 194-246.

Dawson, P., *Organisational Change – A Processual Approach*, London, Paul Chapman, 1994.

European Foundation for the Improvement of Living and Working Conditions, *Towards new forms of work organisation. Can Europe realise its potential? Results of a survey[1] of direct employee participation in Europe*, Luxembourg, Office for Official Publications of the European Communities, 1997.

Gunnarsson, E., 'Women and men – different rationalities?' in E. Gunnarsson and L. Trojer (eds), *Feminist Voices on Gender, Technology and Ethics,* Luleå, University of Technology Centre for Women's Studies, 1994.

Hegewisch, A., van Ommeren, J., Brewster, C., and Kessler, I., European Foundation for the Improvement of Living and Working Conditions, *Direct participation in the social public services*, Luxembourg, Office for Official Publications of the European Communities, 1998.

Kern, H. and Schumann, M., *Das Ende der Arbeitsteilung? Rationaliserung in der industriellen Produktion,* Munich, Beck, 1984.

Piore, M. J. and Sabel, C. F., *The Second Industrial Divide: Possibilities for Prosperity*, New York, Basic Books, 1984.

Storey, J. (ed), *New Wave Manufacturing Strategies – Organisational and Human Resource Management Dimensions,* London, Paul Chapman, 1994.

Woodfield, R., *An ethnographic exploration of some factors which mediate the relationship between gender and skill in a software R&D unit,* University of Sussex, D.Phil thesis, 1994.

---

[1] The EPOC survey.

Chapter 5   Training and Qualifications

The European Commission's (1997) Green Paper, *Partnership for a New Organisation of Work*, is one of a number of recent reports and policy documents which emphasise the importance of skills, knowledge and expertise in the conduct of work within the 'knowledge-based economy' (see also Piore and Sabel 1984; Heisig and Littek, 1995; Andreasen et al, 1995; OECD, 1995; HLEG, 1997). The application of knowledge is regarded as increasingly important in the production of contemporary and increasingly specialised goods and services. It is seen as being vital for the maintenance of competitive advantage in manufacturing industries, since goods and products acquire a higher design and technology content and since processes demand continuous improvement (Womack, Jones and Roos, 1990). In service sectors, a growing emphasis on innovation and on improved responsiveness to customer demand is equally creating pressure for processes and products with a greater 'knowledge-content' (Hauknes and Miles, 1996). The EPOC Research Group report identifies four areas in which skills and knowledge in the workforce are used in a knowledge-based economy:

- to overcome problems in highly automated production processes;
- to effect continuous improvements in work processes and product quality;
- to plan tasks and allocate work; and
- to overcome problems raised by technical and organisational changes.

In this vision of the knowledge-based economy, however, attention is rarely paid to the question of equality of access to knowledge and expertise amongst different groups of employees. Skills and knowledge are generally seen as objective requirements of the work to be performed, rather than attributes of employees which are acquired through social processes of negotiation and reward allocation as well as through training and education. It is therefore commonly assumed that knowledge-based work is equally the domain of all employees working in sectors or industries which rely on the skills and expertise of the workforce.

This assumption is all the more surprising given the way in which skills and qualifications are socially constructed and allocated. As we noted in Chapter 3, skilled work and skilled status are not the equal province of male and female employees. Since the process of industrialisation, the status and rewards attached to 'skill' have been strenuously struggled over, and skilled employees have striven to maintain the exclusivity of such status and rewards. As both Cockburn (1983) and Arnold and Faulkner (1985) have shown in some detail, male craft workers have in the past resolutely fought to exclude women from access to the apprenticeships and training possibilities which would have secured them a decent living. The label of 'skill' must, consequently, be seen as being as much a function of the power and bargaining muscle as of the technical competence or expertise of the employees who possess it.

This inequality of access to skill persists. Women, as we have already noted, are concentrated and segregated in organisations and industries where the possibilities for the use of skill are not as extensive as for male employees based in male-dominated or exclusively male sectors. In manufacturing industries, women are predominantly found in semiskilled areas, while in service organisations they remain overrepresented in routine functions. Moreover, and perhaps more importantly, throughout the economy women remain concentrated in the lower echelons of organisations, where the opportunities for skill and expertise utilisation are inferior to those open to employees in the higher echelons. It also seems that, in processes of innovation and technological change, women's work in many areas of the economy is being persistently rendered routine and deprived of knowledge content (Webster, 1996).

This inequality of access to skill is a feature of the EPOC survey organisations too. In Chapter 3 of this report, we saw how low qualification work was most likely to be a feature of female-dominated than of other types of workplaces, while high qualification work was more common in male-dominated establishments. This pattern was also identified in the report of the EPOC Research Group: the report shows that even in male-dominated areas of the economy in which skill requirements are low, it is the presence of women in the labour force which lowers them, and that conversely, in sectors where skill requirements are high, it is the presence of men in the workforce that raises them. The higher the share of women in workplaces, the lower the qualification requirements and skill orientation (EFILWC, 1997, p. 190). The 'knowledge economy' is, it would seem, only beneficial to sections of the workforce, and the ability to participate fully in it has a strong gender dimension. To what extent might the practice of direct participation promote equal opportunities in the acquisition and exercise of skill and knowledge at work?

The EPOC survey examined the ways in which organisations prepare for direct participation in the training of their employees. Propensity to train provides an indicator of managements' intentions to introduce complex forms of direct participation. The duration of training and the topics on which the workforce is trained also provide indicators of the quality of group delegation and group consultation. There is potential for the achievement of equal opportunities objectives here. Direct participation could be used to improve the conditions and circumstances within which women work, and their prospects for personal development at work. Specifically, the opportunity for women to utilise discretion and to take decisions about the conduct of their work would be important for their knowledge development and general empowerment. This would also improve their job satisfaction. The question is whether direct participation can develop this potential and under what conditions (Goldmann et al, 1994).

The tables which follow examine the training patterns of workplaces engaged in, first, group consultation and, second, group delegation. We have focussed particularly on training for these forms of direct participation because the social dimensions of these aspects of direct participation are particularly important, and gender has already been identified as central to the construction of social skills. It is worth noting, however, that the data collected and presented do not allow us to identify the skills and training opportunities enjoyed by individual employees in the EPOC survey; rather, they show patterns of training for direct participation practised by establishments of different gender compositions. We cannot specify, however, which employees within those establishments are gaining access to training for direct participation. Nor can we determine whether there are differences in access to training between establishments which practise direct participation and those which do not, since, in relation to the training question, the EPOC survey data focuses only on those establishments which do practise direct participation.

Training for group consultation

In the survey overall, only about 50% of workplaces which applied group consultation arrangements provided special training courses for their employees (EFILWC, 1997, p. 177). Many managers declared that they saw investment in training as significant, but much fewer actually put these declarations into practice by offering training courses.

Key findings
- There are no appreciable gender differences in access to training for group consultation.
- Male-dominated workplaces predominate in establishments training for data collection and presentation skills.
- Women have greatest access to training for interpersonal skills and for group dynamics; these forms of training are not evenly distributed between the sexes.

Table 5.1 *Training for group consultation by the gender composition of establishments*

provision of training	\multicolumn{4}{c}{gender composition of establishment}	
	male-only	male-dominated	mixed	female-dominated	average
training provided	38	54	52	50	50
training not provided	62	45	48	50	50
total (n)	100 (491)	100 (875)	100 (736)	100 (577)	100 (2679)

Table 5.1 shows that on average, regardless of gender composition, roughly equal numbers of establishments train and do not train for group consultation. Lack of training seems to be evenly spread among all types of establishments, except in male-only workplaces, which are by far the least likely to train their workforces. Equally, of the establishments which do offer training for group consultation, male-dominated workplaces are less likely than the others to offer their employees any training.

All of these results have, however, to be treated with caution; we found no relationship between training and gender composition of establishment. Half of the establishments which both practise group consultation and employ women in the largest occupational group provide training for their workforce, and this is not affected by the proportion of women in the workforce. But we do not know whether the male and female members of the workforce in these establishments have equality of access to training, simply that training is provided overall. To explore the issue further, we can examine the dynamics of gender in establishments which do and do not train. Are these establishments simultaneously expanding or contracting their female labour forces, and with what implications for women's access to training? Table 5.2 shows establishments which train and do not train by whether they are expanding their male employees as a proportion of their total workforces ('masculising') or expanding their female employees as a proportion of the total ('feminising').

Table 5.2 *Training for group consultation by feminisation or masculisation of establishments*

	establishments increasing % of male employees	establishments increasing % of female employees	total (n)
training	66	34	100 (308)
no training	76	24	100 (331)

This table shows that establishments which train their workforces for group consultation are slightly more likely to simultaneously feminise those workforces than those which do not train. Although these figures support an interesting **suggestion** that establishments may be improving women's access to training in feminising their workforces, our data are not strong enough for such a suggestion to be confidently adopted. Furthermore, the data do not show the inner workings of these establishments, in particular whether the women in these feminising and training establishments are involved in direct participation in proportion to their involvement in training.

In Table 5.3, we consider the topics on which workforces are trained for group consultation by the gender composition of the establishments which are practising group consultation. Establishments identified four topics on which they offer training: data collection and analysis, presentation skills, interpersonal skills, and group dynamics. In the EPOC literature review by Fröhlich and Pekruhl (1996), the social dimension of group activities was particularly emphasised, and thus, so were the social skills requirements they implied. Social skills, of course, have a strong gender dimension. It is something of a commonplace that women possess particularly good social skills (though the source of these skills is variously seen as biologically determined by women's particular linguistic abilities, or, on the other hand, socially acquired through an 'apprenticeship in womanhood'). 'Emotional labour' (using diplomacy, negotiating with people and managing feelings in the workplace); 'rendering a service' (interacting with customers and others inside and outside firms); and performing 'caring tasks' (taking responsibility for maintaining good social relations in the workplace), are all forms of social skill which are associated with the work that women often do, yet they are often unrecognised as 'skills' in the formal sense when performed by women. Indeed, paradoxically, Woodfield has shown that in some settings, these types of skill are only recognised as such when they are used by men, in which case they are seen as primary and productive to the enterprise. By contrast, when used by women, they are seen as secondary and supportive (Woodfield, 1994), and this suggests that the activities done by women are often devalued precisely because of the sex of those who perform them. Do establishments of different gender structures provide equivalent group consultation training for men and women in interpersonal skills and in group dynamics, and with what implications for equal opportunities?

Table 5.3 *Topic of training for group consultation by gender composition of establishment*

topic of training	gender composition of establishment				
	male-only	male-dominated	mixed	female-dominated	average
data collection and analysis	35	31	25	17	27
presentation skills	16	23	23	24	22
interpersonal skills	23	28	30	34	29
group dynamics	26	18	22	25	22
total (n)	100 (356)	100 (940)	100 (768)	100 (689)	100 (2752)

Table 5.3 indicates that there are gender inequalities in access to training in data collection. Male-only and male-dominated establishments make up the clear majority of those providing training on this topic, which may partly reflect the sectors in which such establishments predominate (such as manufacturing, where workforce skill is required in data collection for process control and improvement). However, training in interpersonal skills is more often provided in female-dominated establishments. Training in presentation skills and in group dynamics is much more evenly distributed between workplaces of different gender compositions, suggesting that both men and women are trained in these areas to virtually similar extents. Male-only establishments are slightly

different, in that they provide less training on presentation skills and more on group dynamics. This may well be related to the industry sectors in which such establishments are typically to be found.

Women have no particular advantage of access to training on data collection and analysis, presentation skills, or group dynamics. However, neither are they in any way disadvantaged in their access to these types of training. Looking at the figures particularly for female-dominated workplaces, however, it is clear that the majority train their workforces in interpersonal skills. This suggests that interpersonal skills are still seen as the most relevant type of skill for female employees, and given that training is provided as part and parcel of the move to direct participation, it is clearly seen as a productive factor. This may conceivably be positive for women seeking recognition for the skills which they exercise in the course of their work. Table 5.4 shows in statistical terms[1] no strong gender dimension to the duration of training offered in the past year. Regardless of gender composition, the majority of workplaces offered from one to five days' training, with male-dominated and mixed-sex workplaces forming the majority of establishments offering this length of training.

Table 5.4 *Duration of training for group consultation by gender composition of establishments providing such training*

duration of training	gender composition of establishment				
	male-only	male-dominated	mixed	female-dominated	average
less than 1 day	13	6	8	4	7
1 day	24	17	23	15	19
1-5 days	50	54	58	54	54
5+ days	12	23	20	27	20
total	100	100	100	100	100
(n)	(158)	(398)	(341)	(229)	(1128)

Male-only establishments are more likely to provide less than one day's or one day's training than are other establishments. Female-dominated establishments, by contrast, are least likely to offer less than one day's training and are most likely to offer more than five days' training. It would seem, therefore, that female workforces do not have particular access to training for direct participation, but neither are they unduly discriminated against in training provision. Rather, where female employees are involved in group consultation, they seem to have similar access to training to their male counterparts. There is

---

[1] See the measurements of association provided in the Appendix.

no evidence, therefore, to suggest that training for group consultation is being pressed into the service of equal opportunities objectives, in terms of being used as a mechanism for overcoming gender disadvantage in the workplace. On the other hand, neither is it operating as a mechanism which opens the gender gap wider.

Training for group delegation

We also examined similar gender dimensions of training for group delegation. Group delegation involves the exercise of much more discretion and autonomy in the course of working than does group consultation. Rather than simply working on tasks for a limited period or discussing work-related topics on an ongoing basis, employees are expected to carry out common tasks on a permanent basis without constant reference back to their managers. This suggests that training might be an even more central aspect of group delegation than of group consultation. However, in the EPOC survey, the dynamics of group delegation in general are very similar to those for group consultation: 46% of establishments practising group delegation offer training in preparation for it, and mostly on courses of 1-5 days' duration (EFILWC, 1997, p. 180). As a consequence, the following analysis is based on a relatively small subgroup of establishments in the survey, with the result that some of the figures presented are too small to allow for confident conclusions to be drawn from them.

Table 5.5 *Training for group delegation by the gender composition of the establishments*

duration of training	gender composition of establishment					
	male-only	male-dominated	mixed	female-dominated	average
training	33	48	50	40	43
no training	67	52	50	60	67
total (n)	100 (1200)	100 (1599)	100 (1263)	100 (1201)	100 (5298)

In contrast to the situation for group consultation, in relation to group delegation male-dominated and mixed-sex establishments are most likely to provide training for their employees, and male-only establishments are the least likely to do so. However, the gender differences are too minor to be conclusive, and in the case of non-training establishments, the differences are even slighter. An examination of training for group delegation by feminisation and masculisation of establishments revealed even smaller total numbers, which do not allow for any reliable conclusions at all to be drawn.

Training and Qualifications

Table 5.6 *Topic of training for group delegation by gender composition of establishment*

topic of training	\multicolumn{5}{c}{gender composition of establishment}
	male- only	male- dominated	mixed	female- dominated	average
data collection and analysis	36	28	20	18	24
presentation skills	22	30	35	26	30
interpersonal skills	20	20	20	26	21
group dynamics	22	22	25	31	25
total (n)	100 (186)	100 (502)	100 (455)	100 (301)	100 (1444)

The gender dimensions of the topics in which workforces are trained for group delegation are very similar to those operating for training in preparation for group consultation. Training in data collection and analysis seems to be offered most frequently in male-dominated establishments and least frequently in female-dominated ones; as with group consultation, we believe that this is a function of industry sector and that data collection is used most by employees in manufacturing companies to assist with process control. In services, where women are more dominant, data collection is clearly a much less critical part of the practice of group delegation. Other training topics seem to be most prevalent in male-dominated and mixed-sex workplaces (these were the major trainers in group dynamics), and least prevalent in male-only workplaces. Again, it would seem that where group delegation is introduced in settings where women work, then the training offered to employees is more in what we might call the 'soft' skills necessary for direct participation – interpersonal and group skills – rather than the 'hard' skills with a technical component. The data does not, however, reveal a systematic association in this respect, so we cannot conclude that training for group delegation actively perpetuates conventional gender relations at work. Nor do we know exactly who within the workforce is being trained. Nevertheless, we can see that this training does not appear to confront and overturn these gender stereotypes. The gender typing of jobs, whereby men become associated with technical skills and women with interpersonal and emotional ones, has not been put to the challenge by the practice of group delegation, and in this sense an opportunity for addressing equality objectives has been missed[2].

---

[2] See the statistics provided in the Appendix.

Table 5.7 *Duration of training for group delegation by gender composition of establishments providing such training*

duration of training	gender composition of establishment				
	male-only	male-dominated	mixed	female-dominated	average
less than 1 day	18	5	3	6	7
1 day	18	17	30	15	21
1-5 days	51	56	52	55	54
5+ days	13	20	16	25	19
total (n)	100 (10)	100 (274)	100 (244)	100 (170)	100 (796)

As with group consultation, most workplaces, regardless of gender composition, train their workforces for between one and five days. This aside, there are greater gender differences between establishments training for group delegation than between those training for group consultation. Male-only establishments are the most likely to train for less than one day and the least likely to train for more than this. A single day's training is most likely to be provided in mixed-sex workplaces, and lengthier periods of training are most likely to take place in male-dominated settings. It is worth noting, too, that female-dominated workplaces are much better represented amongst those offering longer than a single day's training than male-only workplaces are, and they are the second most important group offering more than five days' training. In the amount of training given for group delegation, therefore, it seems that there is more discernible gender equity than in other aspects of training.

Key findings
- Mixed-sex establishments are most likely to train for group delegation and male-only establishments are least likely to do so.
- Training for group delegation does not appear to challenge conventional gender stereotypes: training in 'hard' skills is mostly offered in male-dominated settings, while 'soft' human skills training is most prevalent in female-dominated environments.
- The duration of training for group delegation shows a gender dimension, with male-dominated establishments providing the longest training. Female-dominated establishments are also important providers of longer training periods.

Summary and conclusions

The key concern of this chapter has been to explore the issue of whether access to training for direct participation is gender equitable, and to what extent such access might help to promote equal opportunities in the acquisition and exercise of skills and knowledge at work. For this reason, we have concentrated on training provision for employees rather than for managers; despite some recent female inroads into this category of work, the majority of women are concentrated in much lower-level positions within European workplaces and it is these women who are most in need of support through equal opportunities-motivated actions. Women managers, we would argue, have, as individuals, already succeeded in breaking through many of the most long-established obstacles to systematic gender equity in work and employment.

Overall, the length of training to which employees have access varies little between men and women. In other words, men and women train for much the same periods of time, and this is encouraging. It is also something of a surprise: as we have already noted, it is generally assumed that women are concentrated in occupational areas where their access to training is comparatively poor, but the EPOC survey suggests that the women in its establishments do not suffer great disadvantage in this respect. With regard to the duration of training, direct participation does not lead to increasing inequality but at the same time it does not help to overcome the disadvantages of women in working life. However, it is in the topic of training where gender inequality is revealed: some sex typing appears to be taking place in the exposure of men and women to training for particular skill sets. That women are still predominantly trained in 'soft' skills, which help them to function better as employees who smooth the interpersonal relations of the workplace, suggests that some essential assumptions are often made about the training to which they are most appropriately exposed. Yet it is precisely the full range of hard and soft skills which are required if women are to break out of their occupational ghettos and to gain improved equal opportunities of access to different types of work, and this range does not seem to be fully available to them.

In the case of group consultation, there is little difference between workplaces of different gender compositions in their training provision. Although many managers declare training in general to be important, many fewer actually carry that declaration through into practice, and of those that do, most train their workforces for relatively short periods of up to five days. Group consultation is, of course, a relatively weak form of direct participation which does not offer employees extended rights and responsibilities, nor does it appear to be used to develop extensive employee expertise. The survey data do not allow us to judge whether establishments use training as a mechanism for helping them to overcome gender segregation in their workforces, principally because we cannot compare establishments which train for direct participation with those which offer general training, but do not practise direct participation. However, none of the workplaces in the EPOC survey appear to use training for group consultation to promote equal opportunities objectives. To do so would surely involve the conscious application of strategies to redress women's inequality of access to training and perhaps to ensure that female workforces acquire 'non-traditional' skills which allow them to move out of their confinement in 'caring' and service work and into broader occupational areas. There is no reliable evidence in the EPOC survey of this type of strategy having been pursued.

In firms practising group delegation – where systematic strategies for equal opportunities could be effectively pursued – the training scenario is very similar. Female-dominated workplaces fare much the same as male-dominated workplaces in their access to training and in the topics and duration of training. They are slightly more likely to be offered training in human and interpersonal skills and less likely to receive it in technical skills. Here, too, there is no sign of attempts to break down the sexual division of labour.

One further point is worth noting. Of all the different types of workplaces, male-only workplaces are the least well provided for in terms of training for both group consultation and group delegation. They are the least likely to provide training at all, and where they do, they are most likely to provide very short training courses of less than one day. Does this suggest, then, that men have poorer access to training than we have so far suggested?

These male-only establishments are particular types of workplaces, concentrated in the mining and construction sectors. These are sectors which, overall, have low rates of direct participation (EFILWC, 1997, p. 32), and where they do practise direct participation, they seem to do so in a limited way with little training provision. This may partly reflect the fact that techniques such as Total Quality Management, lean production and quality circles are likely to be less relevant in these industries than in manufacturing or even service organisations. Nevertheless, it shows that here are groups of male employees who do not enjoy access to training provision for direct participation and for whom direct participation is quite limited – more along the lines of the 'Toyota' model than the Scandinavian one (EFILWC, 1997, p. 180).

References

Andreasen, L. E., Coriat, B., den Hertog, F., and Kaplinsky, R. (eds), *Europe's Next Step: Organisational Innovation, Competition and Employment,* London, Frank Cass, 1995.

Arnold, E. and Faulkner, W., 'Smothered by invention: the masculinity of technology' in Faulkner, W. and Arnold, E. (eds), *Smothered by Invention: Technology in Women's Lives,* London, Pluto, 1985.

Cockburn, C., *Brothers: Male Dominance and Technological Change,* London, Pluto, 1983.

European Commission, Green Paper, *Partnership for a new organisation of work,* Luxembourg, Office for Official Publications of the European Communities, 1997.

European Foundation for the Improvement of Living and Working Conditions, *New forms of work organisation. Can Europe realise its potential? Results of a survey of direct employee participation in Europe,* Luxembourg, Office for Official Publications of the European Communities, 1997.

Fröhlich, D. and Pekruhl, U., European Foundation for the Improvement of Living and Working Conditions, *Direct participation and organisational change – fashionable but misunderstood? An analysis of recent research in Europe, Japan and the USA,* Luxembourg, Office for Official Publications of the European Communities, 1996.

Goldmann, M., Kutzner, E., Riezler, M., and Aumann, K., *Perspektiven von Frauenarbeit bei neuen Produktions- und Managementkonzepte,* Reihe: Beiträge aus der Forschung, Bd. 76, Dortmund, Sozialforschungsstelle, 1994.

Hauknes, J. and Miles, I., *Services in European Innovation Systems – A Review of Issues,* Oslo, STEP Report, 1996.

Heisig, U. and Littek, W., 'Trust as a basis of work organisation', in Littek, W. and Charles, T. (eds), *The New Division of Labour: Emerging Forms of Work Organisation in International Perspective,* Berlin, Walter de Gruyter, 1995.

HLEG, *Building the European Information Society for Us All*, Final Policy Report of the High Level Expert Group, Luxembourg, Office for Official Publications of the European Communities, 1997.

OECD, *Employment and Growth in the Knowledge-Based Economy*, Paris, OECD, 1995.

Piore, M. J. and Sabel, C, *The Second Industrial Divide: Possibilities for Prosperity*, New York, Basic Books, 1984.

Webster, J., *Shaping Women's Work: Gender, Employment and Information Technology,* London, Longman, 1996.

Womack, J. P., Jones, D. T., and Roos, D., *The Machine that Changed the World*, New York, Rawson Associates, 1990.

Woodfield, R., *An ethnographic exploration of some factors which mediate the relationship between gender and skill in a software R&D unit,* University of Sussex, D.Phil thesis, 1994.

Chapter 6

The Effects of Direct Participation on Equal Opportunities

In Chapter 4, we saw that the practice of direct participation does not have strong gender dimensions – all types of workplaces practise it, though mixed-sex workplaces can be said to be particularly significant and intense practitioners. In other words, direct participation seems to be most in evidence in settings where there is a weak sexual division of labour, or none at all, and where establishments are innovative along other dimensions.

Is this innovative approach to the organisation of work carried further in workplaces practising direct participation? What is direct participation being practised for? What is it being used to achieve? Does it have positive or negative impacts in the settings in which it is used and are these outcomes differentiated by the gender composition of the establishments using it? In this chapter, we examine managements' perceptions of the outcomes of direct participation on the employment, indirect labour costs and economic performance patterns in their organisations, and we consider the implications for equal opportunities for women and men in European workplaces. As the EPOC Research Group's (1997) report makes clear, the data available provide indicators rather than direct answers to these issues. Moreover, the indicators are qualitative rather than quantitative, showing, for example, that establishments have reduced employment but not the number of jobs which have been lost, or whether additional labour has been taken on.

The effects of direct participation

Previous studies and our analysis of the EPOC survey data thus far make it reasonable to assume that the effects of direct participation might be gender differentiated, even if the extent of the practice itself is not. For example, over the years, various studies have suggested that managements' most searching employment rationalisation efforts tend to be directed towards higher labour cost areas (see, for example, Dobb, 1946; Taft, 1963; Thompson, 1983). We may therefore assume that in the EPOC survey workplaces, male-dominated establishments are more likely than female-dominated ones to show reductions in employees and also in managers.

Key findings
- Direct participation has no influence on the gender composition of establishments.
- Among all practitioners of direct participation, male-dominated and mixed-sex establishments are slightly more likely to reduce their proportion of female staff than are other establishments.
- Male-dominated establishments are most likely to report both positive (improved economic performance) and negative (job reduction) effects of direct participation.

Table 6.1 *The influence of direct participation on the gender composition of establishments*

practice of direct participation	male-only	male-dominated	mixed-sex	female-dominated	total (n)
establishment practises:					
at least one form of DP	21	30	27	22	100 (4286)
no form of DP	30	28	18	24	100 (990)
average	23	30	25	23	100 (5276)

Table 6.1 shows that direct participation has little or no influence on the gender composition of establishments. Although mixed-sex establishments are more prevalent among those practising direct participation than among those not practising it, we cannot conclude from this that direct participation therefore results in a more gender equitable division of labour within those establishments. Unfortunately, we have no information about the precise sexual division of labour within the EPOC survey establishments, or about the way this is shaped. While we can hope that direct participation might act as a factor in reducing gender inequalities in organisations, there are many other factors which preserve and reinforce such inequalities (such as the ongoing dynamics of vertical and horizontal segregation by sex), and these have to set against any possible positive effects of direct participation.

The Effects of Direct Participation on Equal Opportunities

Table 6.2 *The influence of direct participation on changes in the gender composition of establishments*[1]

practice of direct participation	change in gender composition of establishment		
	de-feminisation	feminisation	total (n)
establishment practises at least one form of direct participation	76	24	100 (1275)
establishment practises no form of direct participation	69	31	100 (195)

We can only meaningfully analyse the effects of direct participation on the gender composition of establishments by examining changes in the numbers of women and men **relative to the total workforce** in the EPOC survey establishments. (These are the variables of 'feminisation' and 'de-feminisation' which we have described in Chapter 2 of this report. They are much more effective indicators of changing gender composition than a simple measure of change in the absolute number of women regardless of change in workforce size. 'De-feminisation' indicates that the share of women in the workforce has decreased, while 'feminisation' indicates that the share has increased.) Contrary to hopes for the potentially gender equitable outcomes of direct participation, Table 6.2 shows that establishments practising direct participation are actually slightly more likely to de-feminise their labour forces than those which do not practise direct participation. However, the numbers reported in this table are small, so should be taken with caution.

Table 6.3 shows the different outcomes of direct participation which were reported by the establishments in the EPOC survey, differentiated by the gender composition of the establishments. The variables – 'cost reduction', 'reduction of throughput times', 'improvement of quality of production or service', and 'increase in total output' – are indicators of **economic performance**. In general, these effects were reported by a relatively large number of managers, and the EPOC Research Group has therefore pointed to the positive effects of direct participation on economic performance.

Differentiating those establishments by their gender composition, it is clear that improved economic performance is most likely to occur in male-dominated establishments, although quality improvements are almost as important in mixed-sex settings. Cost reduction and reduction of throughput times are most

---
[1] The numbers are too small to allow a further breakdown by sector or occupation.

clearly gender-differentiated and male-dominated. It is interesting to note that, of the female-dominated establishments, more than 50% report no economic performance improvements of these kinds. We assume that these establishments are predominantly in the public services sector, and therefore undertake other forms of restructuring than those favoured by firms in manufacturing or in private services[2]. This is reasonable because the EPOC Research Group report shows that economic performance improvements are associated with all forms of direct participation, but particularly with group delegation. On this basis, it is not unreasonable to assume that these establishments are likely to be predominantly in the manufacturing sector, and that they are likely to be those types of organisations which are introducing group work or similar innovations in the context of broader 'lean production' strategies for inventory reduction and lead-time improvements (Womack et al, 1990; Wickens, 1987).

Table 6.3 *Economic effects of direct participation by gender composition of establishments*

| | gender composition of establishment |||| |
reported effect of direct participation	male-only	male-dominated	mixed	female-dominated	total (n)
cost reduction	67	71	62	45	62 (1391)
throughput times reduced	60	78	65	46	64 (1387)
production/service quality improved	90	93	95	90	92 (2634)
increase in total output	52	57	50	33	50 (910)

Table 6.4 *Social and employment effects of direct participation by gender composition of establishment*

| | gender composition of establishment |||| |
reported effect of direct participation	male-only	male-dominated	mixed	female-dominated	total (n)
decrease in sickness	35	32	33	36	34 (616)
decrease in absenteeism	35	34	32	42	36 (647)
employees nos. reduced	22	34	34	27	30 (524)
no. managers reduced	19	27	26	16	22 (373)

---

[2] See Table 6A6 and Table 6A7 in the Appendix. However the differences between the two Tables should not be overemphasised. Partly, the numbers within the cells are very small, and we also have no comparative information about those establishments which do not practise direct participation.

Table 6.4 shows the gender dimensions of two indicators of improvements in **indirect labour costs** – decrease in sickness and decrease in absenteeism. Overall, fewer establishments reported these phenomena as effects of direct participation than economic performance improvements and it seems that direct participation is nowadays principally an organisational development tool used to influence output, throughput time and quality (EFILWC, 1997, p. 111). However, these effects are much more evenly reported by the establishments of different gender compositions, with male-only and female-dominated establishments reporting these effects to almost the same extent as male-dominated and mixed-sex establishments. Indeed, slightly more female-dominated than male-dominated establishments reported a decrease in sickness and absenteeism.

Finally, in Table 6.4, we note the effects of direct participation on **employment reduction** in establishments of different gender compositions. Overall, and regardless of the gender dimension, group consultation, group delegation and particularly arm's length consultation were the forms of direct participation most strongly linked to employment reduction. Although, as we have already noted, we are not able to differentiate the forms of direct participation and their effects by the gender composition of establishments in a way which would allow us to draw conclusive results, Table 6.4 shows that the male-dominated establishments are those most affected by employment reduction, both of employees and of managers. In the case of employee reduction, it is interesting to note that male-only establishments were those which reported this effect the least; this may be an indication of an industry sector effect, with the greatest incidence of employee reduction being experienced in manufacturing and the lowest incidence being in sectors like construction and mining. Again, the number of responses on the effects of DP does not allow us to differentiate industry sector by gender composition of establishments in a meaningful and detailed enough way. In the case of reduction of managers, female-dominated establishments were the least affected, perhaps because they are mainly in sectors which are not pursuing 'delayering' strategies. Another explanation for this result is simply that female-dominated establishments which also have female managers are a comparative rarity in the first place (though the EPOC survey data do not reveal the sex of the establishments' managers). Employment reduction then, is, as we expected, a strategy which is used more commonly for streamlining male workforces than female ones, and is probably related to the higher labour costs and therefore greater potential cost savings attaching to the former. The EPOC survey data seem to support the findings of previous research in this area.

Summary and conclusions

The reported effects of direct participation, particularly those shown in Table 6.3, should be treated with some caution. More than half of the establishments which reported the practice of direct participation did not, however, answer the EPOC survey question on the **effects** of practising direct participation. It is very probable that only those establishments which experienced positive outcomes of direct participation reported any effects at all, and this of course somewhat skews the picture we have. Furthermore, the associations which do emerge from the survey results are quite weak and based on very small numbers. The results of this chapter should be treated with caution because there is no information of how establishments not practising direct participation perform economically and with regard to indirect labour costs.

The number of responses to the issue of the effects of direct participation place considerable limitations on our ability to disaggregate these effects by the gender composition of the establishments and by the form, scope or combination of forms of direct participation practised. Nevertheless, with the exception of indirect labour cost reductions, and with the caveats mentioned above, we can identify a gender dimension to the effects of direct participation. Male-dominated establishments are most likely to report improvements in economic performance on the one hand, but also employment reduction on the other. Female-dominated establishments are the least likely to report improvements in economic performance.

This suggests that the organisations which we identified in the previous chapter as possible innovators (i.e. those which are the most important practitioners of direct participation and which are of mixed sex) are not the most significant pursuers of economic performance improvements (through lean production or other arrangements, with the exception of quality improvements which might reflect teamworking initiatives). In other words, with this exception, they do not appear to be the most active in seeking performance improvements as a result of their approaches to a mixed-sex workforce and to the practice of direct participation. We cannot, therefore, conclude that there is a cohort of organisations in the EPOC survey which is fundamentally innovative both in gender terms and in organisational strategy, and which is pursuing such a strategy to effect economic performance improvements.

Instead, the most frequent reporters of both positive and negative effects of direct participation are male-dominated organisations, and this simple finding itself has implications for equal opportunities. For the pursuance by organisations of strategies for improved economic performance often entails retraining and the use of new skills on the part of the labour – for example, in teamworking, in self-management, and in intergroup communications, and it would therefore seem that women are not significant beneficiaries of these initiatives in the EPOC survey workplaces. We can thus conclude, from the data available, that there are no positive equal opportunities outcomes of direct participation, in the sense of women in significant numbers in organisations taking part in programmes for improved economic performance, which in turn may require the acquisition and exercise of new, transferrable skills and knowledge for their successful implementation. It would seem from this that the potential equal opportunities gains to be had from the practice of direct participation are much slighter than some of the more optimistic forecasts have suggested. We draw some conclusions for equal opportunities from the survey findings in the next chapter.

References

Dobb, M., *Studies in the Development of Capitalism*, London, Routledge, 1946.

European Foundation for the Improvement of Living and Working Conditions, *New forms of work organisation. Can Europe realise its potential? Results of a survey of indirect employee participation in Europe,* Luxembourg, Office for Official Publications of the European Communities, 1997.

Taft, P., 'Organized labor and technical change: a backward look', in Somers, G., Cushman, E. L. and Weinberg, N. (eds), *Adjusting to Technological Change*, New York, Harper and Row, 1963.

Thompson, P., *The Nature of Work*, London, Macmillan, 1983.

Wickens, P., *The Road to Nissan: Flexibility, Quality, Teamwork*, London, Macmillan, 1987.

Womack, J. P., Jones, D. T., and Roos, D., *The Machine that Changed the World*, New York, Rawson Associates, 1990.

Chapter 7

Summary, Conclusions and Future Directions

One of the key features of European organisations is the relative position of men and women within them and within the labour market generally. The sexual division of labour is something which often tends to be overlooked in discussions of organisational change. But our analysis of the EPOC survey workplaces shows that there are important equal opportunities issues raised by innovations in Europe's workplaces. In this chapter, we summarise our findings and present a discussion of issues which we believe warrant further attention.

Key findings

- Although men and women are equally involved in the practice of direct participation, this equal involvement takes place within a context of pronounced horizontal and vertical occupational segregation of the sexes. Women are found in particular industries and occupations, often with poorer working conditions than their male counterparts. For example, low-skilled work is much more likely to be a characteristic of female-dominated establishments than of other types of establishment. Similarly, workplaces employing women in large proportions are especially likely to accentuate their reliance on part-time work.
- Mixed-sex establishments are the most active practitioners of direct participation. They are most likely to practise multiple forms of it, and to practise high intensity direct participation. These establishments are therefore implementing suites of organisational changes and should be encouraged to take the opportunity to simultaneously improve equal opportunities.

- Despite this potentially promising scenario, there is no evidence of direct participation being practised with the objective of pressing home equal opportunities programmes in Europe's workplaces. It is not used as an instrument to overcome gender segregation in jobs and working conditions.
- Training provision for direct participation indicates that equal opportunities objectives are not being strongly pursued. Training is generally provided along somewhat gender stereotyped lines: training in technical skills is mostly offered in male-dominated settings, while 'soft' human skills training is most prevalent in female-dominated environments.

The EPOC survey – a methodology for gender analysis

The key methodological points can be summarised as follows:

- The basis of the analysis of the gender dimensions of direct employee participation is a secondary analysis of the EPOC survey data.
- Ten countries were involved in the EPOC survey: Denmark, France, Germany, Ireland, Italy, the Netherlands, Portugal, Spain, Sweden and the United Kingdom. Respondents were workplace general managers or the manager deemed most appropriate: the focus was the workplace's largest occupational group. Statistically, this group of employees can be seen as a valid proxy for the whole workforce. The unit of analysis was the workplace and its largest occupational group. Employees as individuals or their interactions were not the subject of the survey.
- In order to examine the sexual division of labour in the survey establishments, a measure of the gender composition of the largest occupational group was developed. Establishments were differentiated according to the proportion of women in their largest occupational group.

Central questions

The report presents an analysis of the 1996 EPOC survey data as they relate to the gender composition of European workplaces and their use of direct participation. The report hinges on two key aspects of direct participation and equal opportunities: first, equality of access to direct participation, and second, the effects of direct participation on equal opportunities and particularly on gender segregation in European workplaces. The report starts by examining the overall characteristics of these workplaces, and thus the conditions in which men and women are employed. This initial discussion provides the context within which the practice of direct participation is considered. The patterns of direct participation practised in workplaces of different gender composition are scrutinised, and thus the opportunities for the two sexes to be involved in direct participation are explored. The second part of the analysis concentrates on the effects of direct participation on the training provided to employees, on employment itself and on economic performance in organisations of different gender compositions. This provides an indication of the equal opportunities outcomes of direct participation.

The gender composition of the EPOC establishments

The gender structures of the EPOC workplaces confirm the established contention that women are segregated in a relatively narrow range of industry sectors and in a few occupational groups, and that there are significant areas of the economy where women are not found at all. Moreover, developments in 'atypical employment' (the growth of part-time work, temporary work, subcontracting and other forms of 'flexible' employment) are firmly gendered. Part-time employment contracts are growing particularly rapidly in areas where women work, whilst temporary work is growing in establishments where both sexes work.

The key factor shaping the presence and position of women is industry sector, and women's presence in companies with particular characteristics is related to the fact that these companies are in sectors in which women are strongly represented. In addition, repetitious and routine work seems to be more associated with female-dominated employment, and firms which make strong use of female labour seem to be less likely to make capital investments, perhaps because they have less need to than those which employ still relatively expensive male labour. Finally, women are employed in jobs which require lower skills and qualifications than jobs in which men are found.

These findings have important implications for women's access to direct participation and their ability to benefit from processes of direct participation. They raise questions about whether women are located in sectors and jobs in which direct participation is practised, and about whether direct participation alters their conditions of work, their access to skills and training, and indeed their employment segregation.

Direct participation and gender

Women's involvement in direct participation is surely an important indicator of the effectiveness of those practices, particularly in fulfilling an equal opportunities agenda. The report considers the extent to which women are involved, before examining whether their involvement translates into positive workplace reorganisation initiatives which prioritise equal opportunities at work.

Overall, 81% of the EPOC workplaces report the practice of direct participation. 86% of practitioners are mixed-sex establishments, which therefore have above average levels of direct participation. Female-dominated establishments conform to the average level of practice, with almost 80% practising direct participation. This distribution makes mixed-sex establishments the most assiduous practitioners of direct participation, and by implication, women within these establishments are involved in direct participation initiatives. Mixed-sex workplaces are also important practitioners of all forms of direct participation, second only to male-dominated establishments. They are leading practitioners of face-to-face individual consultation, probably because this involves techniques which are widely used in the public sector where mixed-sex workforces are particularly dominant. They are also, importantly, leading practitioners of multiple (between four and six) forms of direct participation, and lead in the practice of high scope participation.

Besides identifying the most active practitioners of direct participation according to their gender structure, we found that direct participation does not disturb established sectoral and occupational gender divisions of labour.

However, looking more closely at the gender composition of groups involved in group consultation and delegation specifically, we find that around one-quarter of establishments either exclude women from these groups altogether, or do not include them in proportion to their overall participation in the labour force. Under-representation takes place in 14% of all establishments practising group consultation, while women are excluded in 13% of the cases. In 13% of the establishments women are underrepresented in group delegation, and they are excluded in 12% of these establishments. Over-representation takes place only in 8% of establishments practising group consultation and in 7% of those providing group delegation. So, despite the importance of mixed-sex workplaces as practitioners of direct participation, their female employees are not always properly or fully represented in that participation. Since the gender dimensions of group consultation and group delegation follow established sectoral and occupational divisions of labour by gender, direct participation does not lead to increasing inequality but at the same time it does not expressly help to overcome the disadvantages faced by women in working life. Moreover, the qualification requirements in these settings, and in female-dominated settings, are generally low, particularly compared to male-dominated direct participation.

Training and qualifications

Overall, men and women train in preparation for direct participation for much the same periods of time, and this is the encouraging message of this survey. However, it is in the topic of training that gender inequality is revealed, in training for particular skill sets. Women are still predominantly trained in 'soft' skills which are perhaps designed to help them to function better as employees who smooth the interpersonal relations of the workplace. Yet it is precisely the full range of hard and soft skills which are required if improvements in equal opportunity of access to different types of work are to be achieved.

The effects of direct participation on equal opportunities

The data show that direct participation has little or no influence on the gender composition of establishments. Although mixed-sex establishments are more prevalent among those practising direct participation than among those not practising it, we cannot conclude from this that direct participation therefore results in a more gender equitable division of labour within those establishments. Male-dominated establishments are most likely to report improvements in economic performance on the one hand, but also employment reduction on the other. Female-dominated establishments are the least likely to report improvements in economic performance. This simple finding itself has implications for equal opportunities. This is because the pursuance of strategies for improved economic performance often entails retraining and the use of new skills on the part of the labour force, for example, in teamworking, in self-management, and in intergroup communications. Women do not appear to be significant beneficiaries of these initiatives in the EPOC survey workplaces. Neither is the sexual division of labour itself much disrupted in organisations practising direct participation. On the contrary, the survey shows a slight retrenchment of gender segregation with the implementation of direct participation in Europe's workplaces.

Does direct participation address gender disadvantage?

Two major concerns have underpinned our discussion of the gender dimensions of employee participation. First, do women and men enjoy equal access to employee participation? And does direct participation in turn help to break down the sexual division of labour in organisations and to promote gender equity in occupations and working conditions?

Our analysis of the EPOC survey data suggests that while there is no gender inequality in access to direct participation, neither is there much cause for optimism that direct participation may help to redress women's traditional disadvantage in the labour market and in their conditions of work. It is certainly the case that access to direct participation is little differentiated by the gender composition of workplaces. With the caveat that workplaces do not directly equate to workforce members, we can draw the conclusion that if access is not gender differentiated, then men and women probably have largely equal access to direct participation. In other words, there is no evidence of gender 'disadvantage' in access to it. Indeed, direct participation seems to be particularly prevalent in organisations in which women are well represented, especially in the public sector (see also the accompanying report in this series of EPOC analyses on *Direct Participation in Social Public Services*). But of course, it is only at the level of the establishments that we find no difference in access to direct participation, and this level of analysis does not tell us whether male and female employees within establishments are treated equally. Indeed, when we scrutinised the coverage of direct participation within establishments, we found that around 25% did not allow their female employees access to direct participation in proportion to their overall membership of the labour force.

Of course, having equality of access to direct participation is not necessarily a positive thing. Direct participation, as we have seen, can be accompanied by organisational innovations which worsen the quality of working life as well as by those which might improve it; increased productivity, downsizing, and employment reduction, for example, are some of the negative consequences of direct participation as far as employees are concerned. Gender equality is not something that any policy maker or employee representative would strive for in this respect. Even increased employee participation through more positive innovations like quality circles has in certain settings been found to be little more than an enhanced form of social control of employees (Garrahan and Stewart, 1992).

Nor is equality of access a signifier of, or even a route to, gender equity at work. As we have seen, in some contexts it may simply mean equality of exposure to some negative employment developments, and not to positive strategies designed to enhance women's prospects and opportunities for moving into more favourable employment situations. The EPOC data show a very close association between structural characteristics of organisations – industry sector and main occupational group – and their gender composition. Thus, female-dominated establishments are in very specific industry sectors, which involve very different work from male-only or male-dominated establishments. The data confirm what a range of studies of women's employment has already amply demonstrated, namely that the decisive determinants of women's work and working conditions are the industry sectors they work in and the occupations they do. Direct participation does nothing at all to disturb these patterns of women's employment, and particularly their occupational segregation in the lower status, lower skilled, and lower paid areas of employment. It therefore does not address women's overall disadvantage in the labour market, which arises from their occupational and sectoral segregation, because it does not overcome this segregation. Indeed, in equal opportunities policy terms, direct participation can be equated with equal treatment strategies in that both sexes are treated equally within its parameters but the basic inequities between them are left untouched, and indeed, are thus if anything perpetuated (Rees, 1995).

The way forward for employee participation and equal opportunities

Where does this suggest future research effort and policy thinking should be directed? First, it is clear that if we are to understand fully the reasons for women's particular experiences of work and the possible options for improving those experiences, then large-scale trends such as those derived from the EPOC survey need 'colouring in' with more qualitative information about the social and cultural processes at work in organisations. One of the main drawbacks of the EPOC survey data from the point of view of an analysis of the gender dynamics of employee participation is its focus on establishments rather than on employees or their interactions. This means that it has not been possible to examine the processes operating within the survey organisations by which sexual divisions of labour have been established and reproduced; jobs and work have been allocated to different employees; gender roles have been set and different forms of rewards have been distributed (Ridgeway, 1997). To some extent, these processes can be examined in quantitative and structural terms, provided that the research instruments used allow for an examination of employees themselves. For example, we know that the work setting and the numbers of men in different employment environments are major factors determining women's experiences as minority employees (Kanter, 1977; Wharton and Baron, 1987; Williams, 1989; Yoder, 1991). Indeed, the EPOC survey data itself confirms this point. We have seen that women in male-dominated establishments are particularly disadvantaged in terms of their access to direct participation; about one-third have no access or only participate in small numbers.

Yet a full understanding of the processes of gender segregation and disadvantage at work must address what Downing (1981) has called the 'cultural' as well as the 'calculable'. It must address the making and remaking of gender relations in workplaces, including their dismantling and remantling (Cockburn and Ormrod, 1993), the organisational processes of what Acker (1992) has called 'doing gender'. It must also recognise the differences between different groups of female employees, for not all women experience disadvantage in the same ways and with the same implications. In other words, research and policy must incorporate a recognition that women's workplace situations, and their ability to participate positively in organisational changes, are shaped by several sets of interrelated dynamics. They are shaped by structural factors which place them disproportionately in low-grade employment positions; they are also shaped by historical processes in which men have come to dominate and women have come to be subordinate members of the labour market, and they are shaped by cultural processes which allocate and reallocate meaning and value to those positions in society generally and within individual workplaces. Effective equal opportunities policy must address all these sites of gendering.

Research analysis in support of policy development could start by addressing such dynamics at work in different workplaces, through ethnographic study, through interviews with women and men in organisations, through analysis of employee diaries, and through close examination of intra-firm processes. Indeed, feminist studies of women's work have for some years been underscored by such an approach, and there is now a considerable body of qualitative research into the dynamics and experience of women's employment (see for example, Benet, 1972; Michel, 1975; Barker and Downing, 1980; Cavendish, 1981, West, 1982; Westwood, 1984; Cockburn, 1985; Bradley, 1989; Crompton and Sanderson, 1990; Gadrey, 1993; Webster, 1996; Bianco, 1997). These types of studies have started from very different premises, and as a result have generated a very different picture from that of the EPOC survey. All of them point not to growing equality between the sexes at work, but to continuing gender divisions of labour which are constantly redefined and renegotiated in the context of technological and organisational innovations.

There is also a strong insistence among researchers of women's work and of equal employment opportunities that recognition of the role of women's unpaid work is indispensable to an understanding of their position in paid work. It is impossible to fully grasp the place of women in the sexual division of labour by looking only at firms or organisations as individual entities or in isolation from the institutions of wider society; to do so is to overlook the fact that the position of women within the sexual division of labour, and their continuing confinement within a relatively narrow range of 'sex-typed' occupations, is in part a product of their position in the home. For domestic responsibilities restrict women's ability to participate fully in the labour market, and shape the kind of work for which women are deemed suitable. More than this, women's role in the domestic sphere is often used to confirm and legitimise their marginal status in the labour market. The current growth in part-time work is, as the EPOC survey data reported here has amply demonstrated, particularly salient for women because it allows them to combine paid employment with their domestic responsibilities, including childcare. This is important in a context in which public childcare provision is either non-existent or in decline.

The role of state and social institutions, then, are also critical to an understanding of women's work. Provision of public childcare is one example of how they influence the growth of particular forms of employment and women's ability to take these up. Women's part-time employment varies enormously between the different countries of the European Union, precisely because childcare and indeed employment legislative regimes vary (Rubery et al, 1995). Educational provision also shapes women's employment options and prospects. Ideological and cultural notions of what is 'fit work for women', which operate in a wider social milieu, come into play. The institutions of marriage, the family, and divorce are central to the position of women in the labour market, and the growing participation of women in the labour markets of many countries reflects changes in these institutions. In other words, changes in gender relations outside employment, in society broadly, have a fundamental impact on those within employment.

Effective analysis of, and policy development for, women's employment, then, requires a much stronger synthesis of workplace organisational change and industrial relations research (such as that in the EPOC survey, with gender studies) than has hitherto taken place, and this report has set out to contribute to that project. Conventional organisational change studies have tended to confine their analysis to the unit of the workplace, with the result that they are unable to appreciate the links between the dynamics of workplaces and wider socio-economic developments. As we have seen, in the case of women's employment, these connections really cannot be ignored.

The data captured by the EPOC survey is effectively a snapshot of the status and gender relations of direct participation in European workplaces at a single point. Of particular value to future policy efforts, particularly those concerned with women's employability, would be an analysis of women's employment trajectories over time, on a longitudinal basis. This would improve our understanding of what happens in periods of organisational change to women who do not remain in the workplace under study, but move out to other work or out of employment altogether. It would therefore help to show how women's employability can be improved. The analysis in this report has provided us with a starting point for addressing the gender relations of organisational change in European workplaces. Clearly, however, there are manifold options for developing this work.

References

Acker, J., 'Gendering organizational theory', in Mills, A. J. and Tancred, P. (eds), *Gendering Organizational Analysis*, London, Sage, 1992.

Barker, J. and Downing, H., 'Word processing and the transformation of the patriarchal relations of control in the office', *Capital and Class* 10, 1980, pp. 64-99.

Benet, M. K., *Secretary: an Enquiry into the Female Ghetto*, London, Sidgwick and Jackson, 1972.

Bianco, M. L., *Donne al lavoro*, Torino, Paravia, 1997.

Bradley, H., *Men's Work, Women's Work*, Cambridge, Polity Press, 1989.

Cavendish, R., *Women on the Line*, London, Routledge, 1981.

Cockburn, C., *Machinery of Dominance: Men, Women and Technical Know-How*, London, Pluto Press, 1985.

Cockburn, C. and Ormrod, S., *Gender and Technology in the Making*, London, Sage, 1993.

Crompton, R. and Sanderson, K., *Gendered Jobs and Social Change*, London, Unwin Hyman, 1990.

Downing, H., 'Developments in secretarial labour: resistance, office automation and the transformation of patriarchal relations of control', Birmingham, University of Birmingham, PhD thesis, 1981.

Gadrey, N., *Les Hommes et les Femmes au Travail*, Paris, l'Harmattan, 1993.

Garrahan, P. and Stewart, P., *The Nissan Enigma*, London, Mansell, 1992.

Kanter, R. M., *Men and Women of the Corporation*, New York, Basic Books, 1977.

Michel, A. with Bereaud, S. and Loree, M., *Inégalités professionnelles et socialisation différentielle des sexes*, Paris, Cordes-CNRS, 1975.

Rees, T., *The Position of Women in the EC Training Programmes: Tinkering, Tailoring, Transforming*, Bristol, University of Bristol, Policy Press, 1995.

Ridgeway Cecilia L., 'Interaction and the conservation of gender inequality: considering employment', *American Sociological Review*, Vol. 62, April 1997, pp. 218-235.

Rubery, J., Smith, M., and Fagan, C., *Changing Patterns of Work and Working-Time in the European Union and the Impact on Gender Divisions*, Report for the Equal Opportunities Unit of DGV of the Commission of the European Communities, 1995.

Webster, J., *Shaping Women's Work: Gender, Employment and Information Technology*, London, Longman, 1996.

West, J., *Work, Women and the Labour Market*, London, Routledge and Kegan Paul, 1982.

Westwood, S., *All Day Every Day: Factory and Family in the Making of Women's Lives*, London, Pluto Press, 1984.

Wharton, A. S. and Baron, J. A., 'So happy together? The impact of gender segregation on men at work', *American Sociological Review*, Vol. 52, 1987, pp. 574-587.

Williams, C. L., *Gender Differences at Work: Women and Men in Non-Traditional Occupations*, Berkeley, University of California Press, 1989.

Yoder, J. D., 'Rethinking tokenism: looking beyond numbers', *Gender and Society* 5, 1991, pp. 178-192.

Appendix

Additional statistical information about the tables presented in the text

For readers who are interested in the statistical detail which underlies the findings presented in this report, we present in this Appendix a table of measures of association and their levels of significance.

Since most of the variables we have used for our analysis of the gender dimensions of direct participation are categorical variables, we have used Cramer's V as a measure of association[1]. Where relevant, we have indicated where other types of measures have been used. Although the requirements of significance testing are not fully met because of the relatively high non-response rate in the survey, we nevertheless present the level of significance in the Table below. This Table provides us with a frame of reference for assessing how plausible our results would be under random sampling conditions. In other words, it gives us a first hint of the degree to which the results may be due to chance or are produced systematically. We found that most of our results are significant, but some of them (with small values of the association measurements) have a low level of significance. If third variables are introduced the differences between the indices of compared groups are not tested for their significance.

---

[1] This assumes values between 0 and 1. Values of '0' indicate no correlation or association – the observed variables are independent of each other; values of '1' indicate a perfect dependency or correlation between the two observed variables.

Participating on Equal Terms?

Number of table in text		Cramer's V	Level of significance
	Chapter 2		
2.3		.27	p<.000
2.4		.3	p<.000
2.6		.12	p<.000
	Chapter 3		
3.2		.13	p<.000
3.3		.27[2]	p<.000
Fig. 3.1		.29	p<.000
3.4		.35	p<.000
3.5		.33	p<.000
3.6		.32	p<.000
Fig. 3.2	gender*part-time	.34	p<.000
	gender*temporary contracts	.02	p=.61
Fig. 3.3		.24	p<.000
3.7		.24	p<.000
3.8		.01	p=.73
3.9		.35	p<.000
3.10		.25	p<.000
3.11		Kendall's Tau C: .02	p=.16
3.12		Kendall's Tau C: −.1	p<.000
3.13		Kendall's Tau C: .07	p<.000
Fig. 3.4		.37	p<.000
	Chapter 4		
4.1		.1	p<.000
Fig 4.1		.1[3]	p<.000
4.2	without DP:	.20	p<.000
	with DP:	.14	p<.000
4.3	without DP:	.28	p<.000
	with DP:	.30	p<.000
4.4	without DP:	.33	p<.000
	with DP:	.32	p<.000
4.5	arm's length:	.06	p<.000
	face-to-face:	.11	p<.000
	temp. groups:	.07	p<.000
	perm. groups:	.05	p=.02
	ind. delegation:	.09	p<.000
	group delegation:	.05	p=.05
4.6		.01	p<.000
4.7		Kendall Tau C: .54	p<.000
4.8		Kendall Tau C: .54	p<.000
4.9		Kendall Tau C: .13	p<.000
4.10		.2	p<.000
4.11		Kendall Tau C: 1.3	p<.000

[2] The value equals Table 2.3.
[3] The value equals Table 4.1.

Appendix

Number of table in text		Cramer's V	Level of significance
4.12		.2	p<.000
4.13		Kendall Tau C: .03	p=.01
4.14		Kendall Tau C:	
	arm's length:	.04	p=.05
	face-to-face:	.01	p=.66
	temp. groups:	.04	p=.1
	perm. groups:	.05	p=.006
	ind. delegation:	.06	p=.004
	group delegation:	-.05	p=.016
4.15	working time reduction:	.06	p=.005
	working time flexibility:	.05	p=.02
	downsizing:	.04	p=.05
	outsourcing:	.05	p=.03
	back to core business:	.1	p<.000
	strategic alliances:	.12	p<.000
	product innovation:	.1	p<.000
	new information technology:	.11	p<.000
	automation:	.1	p<.000
4.16	arm's length:	.36	p<.000
	face-to-face:	.40	p<.000
	temp. groups:	.33	p<.000
	perm. groups:	.36	p<.000
	ind. delegation:	.35	p<.000
	group delegation:	.35	p<.000
4.17	arm's length:	.05	p=.216
	face-to-face:	.04	p=.370
	temp. groups:	.02	p=.715
	perm. groups:	.12	p<.000
	ind. delegation:	.12	p<.000
	group delegation:	.03	p=.678
4.18		Kendall Tau C:	
	without DP:	-.09	p=.005
	with DP:	-.1	p<.000
Chapter 5			
5.1		.13	p<.000
5.2		.12	p=.002
5.3	Data collection/analysis:	.12	p<.000
	presentation skills:	.1	p<.000
	interpersonal skills:	.12	p<.000
	group dynamics:	.06	p=.013
5.4		Kendall Tau C: .08	p=.003
5.5		.11	p<.000
5.6	Data collection/analysis:	.12	p<.000
	presentation skills:	.16	p<.000
	interpersonal skills:	.08	p=.014
	group dynamics:	.10	p<.000
5.7		Kendall Tau C: .06	p=.079

Number of table in text	Cramer's V	Level of significance
Chapter 6		
6.1	.14[4]	p<.000
6.2	.05	p=.064
6.3 *has DP*		
cost reduction:	.2	p<.000
reduction of throughput time:	.24	p<.000
improvement of quality:	.09	p<.000
increase in total output:	.14	p<.000
decrease in sickness:	.04	p=.51
decrease in absenteeism:	.08	p=.009
reduction of number of employees:	.11	p<.000
reduction of number of managers:	.12	p<.000
has no DP		
cost reduction:	.20	p=.055
reduction of throughput time:	.10	p=.635
improvement of quality:	.09	p=.615
increase in total output:	.14	p=.428
decease in sickness:	.18	p=.247
decrease in absenteeism:	.12	p=.605
reduction of number of employees:	.17	p=.247
reduction of numbers of manager:	.36	p=.002

Additional tables

Table 3A1: Proportion of establishments of different size and their gender composition
Table 3A2: Increase in number of women by increase of part-time contracts
Table 3A3: Increase in number of women by increase of temporary contracts
Table 3A4: Different levels of qualification required in different sectors
Table 3A5: Increase in number of women in establishments requiring different levels of qualification
Table 3A6: Establishments of different sectors by ownership and profit orientation
Figure 4A1: Plan of the analysis of Chapters 4, 5, and 6
Table 4A1: Gender composition of establishments practising direct participation by form of direct participation practised
Table 4A2: Gender composition of groups in establishments practising direct participation: group consultation (total percentages)
Table 4A3: Gender composition of groups in establishments practising direct participation: group delegation (total percentages)

---

[4] The value equals Table 4.1

Appendix

Table 4A4: Gender coverage of group consultation and gender composition
Table 4A5: Gender coverage of group delegation and gender composition
Table 6A6: Sectorial distribution of establishments reporting the four dimensions of economic performance by their gender structure
Table 6A7: Sectorial distribution of establishments reporting the four dimensions of indirect labour costs by their gender structure

Table 3A1 *Proportion of establishments of different size and their gender composition*

size of establishment (no. of employees)	male-only	male-dominated	mixed	female-dominated	total (n)
–49	27	23	26	24	100 (1162)
50-99	26	29	24	22	100 (1872)
100-199	21	32	24	23	100 (1285)
200-499	17	35	26	22	100 (677)
500+	11	38	29	21	100 (280)
average	23	30	25	23	100 (5276)

* Kandell Tau C: .03, p<.000

Table 3A2 *Increase in number of women by increase in part-time work*

increase in number of women	increase in part-time work		
	yes	no	total (n)
yes	39	61	100 (684)
no	14	86	100 (3521)
average	18	82	100 (4205)

* Cramer's V: .25, p<.000

Table 3A3 *Increase in number of women by increase in temporary work*

increase in number of women	increase in temporary contracts		
	yes	no	total (n)
yes	38	62	100 (612)
no	21	89	100 (3502)
average	23	77	100 (4114)

* Cramer's V: .14, p<.000

Table 3A4 *Establishments of different sectors by ownership and profit orientation*

profit orientation	industry	construction	trade	private services	public services	total (n)
private and profit	47	9	24	16	4	100 (3930)
private and non-profit	8	3	18	14	58	100 (140)
public and profit	18	14	9	22	38	100 (424)
public and non-profit	2	1	3	10	83	100 (681)
average	37	7	20	15	20	100 (5175)

* Cramer's V: .43, p<.000

Table 3A5 *Different levels of qualification required in different sectors*

sector	low	middle	high	total (n)
industry	23	32	45	100 (1813)
construction	16	29	55	100 (339)
trade	29	29	43	100 (969)
private services	24	26	50	100 (749)
public services	14	20	66	100 (1049)

* Cramer's V: .13, p<.000

Table 3A6 *Increase in number of women in establishments requiring different levels of qualification*

qualification requirements	Yes	No	Total (n)
high	17	83	100 (814)
middle	16	84	100 (1033)
low	20	80	100 (1984)
average	19	81	100 (3858)

* Cramer's V: .05, p<.004

Appendix

Figure 4A1 *Plan of the analysis of Chapters 4, 5, and 6*

```
examined in EPOC Research          Direct              examined in Chapter 4, 5,
Group (1997)                   Participation           and 6


            Workplace
          Characteristics                              Gender

                    examined in Chapter 3 of this
                                report
```

Table 4A1 *Gender composition of establishments practising direct participation by form of direct participation practised*[1]

form of direct participation	male-only	male-dominated	mixed	female-dominated	all establishments (n)
arm's length individual consultation	20	33	27	20	100 (2026)
face-to-face individual consultation	18	29	31	22	100 (1876)
temporary group consultation	21	32	28	20	100 (1699)
permanent group consultation	18	31	29	22	100 (1641)
individual delegation	19	30	29	22	100 (2846)
group delegation	20	30	28	22	100 (1722)

[1] For measurements of associations see additional statistical information regarding Table 4.5 on page 134 of this Appendix.

Table 4A2 *Gender composition of groups in establishments practising direct participation: group consultation (total percentages)*

gender composition of group consultation	gender composition of establishment				
	male-only	male-dominated	mixed	female-dominated	all establishments (n)
male-only	17	8	3	2	30
male-dominated	2	20	8	2	32
mixed	0	3	15	4	23
female-dominated	1	0	2	13	16
average	20	32	28	21	100 (2536)

Table 4A3 *Gender composition of groups in establishments practising direct participation: group delegation*

gender composition of group delegation	gender composition of establishment				
	male-only	male-dominated	mixed	female-dominated	all establishments (n)
male-only	16	8	3	1	29
male-dominated	2	19	8	2	31
mixed	0	3	18	3	24
female-dominated	1	0	2	13	16
average	20	30	30	20	100 (1493)

Table 4A4 *Gender coverage of group consultation and gender composition*

gender composition	gender coverage				
	workforce low; women low	workforce high; women low	workforce low; women high	workforce high; women high	all establishments (n)
male-only	72	21	7	0	100 (57)
male-dominated	55	42	2	1	100 (565)
mixed sex	35	19	22	24	100 (611)
female-dominated	11	4	42	43	100 (468)
average (n)	36	23	20	21	100 (1701)

* Cramer's V: .4, p<.000

Appendix

Table 4A5 *Gender coverage of group delegation and gender composition*

gender composition	gender coverage				
	workforce low; women low	workforce high; women low	workforce low; women high	workforce high; women high	all establish-ments (n)
male only	60	30	10	0	100 (30)
male-dominated	46	48	3	3	100 (277)
mixed	30	13	23	35	100 (351)
female-dominated	19	5	42	35	100 (265)
average (n)	32	22	22	24	100 (923)

*Cramer's V: .34, p<.000

Table 6A6 *Sectorial distribution of establishments reporting the four dimensions of economic performance by their gender structure*

sector	gender structure				
	male-only	male-dominated	mixed	female-dominated	average
industry	48	50	29	16	37
construction	20	4	0	0	6
trade	10	16	22	29	19
private sector	13	15	24	13	17
public sector	9	15	26	42	22
total (n)	100 (684)	100 (1016)	100 (894)	100 (690)	100 (3284)

*Cramer's V : .29, p<.000

Table 6A7 *Sectoral distribution of establishments reporting the four dimensions of indirect labour costs by their gender structure*

sector	gender structure				
	male-only	male-dominated	mixed	female-dominated	average
industry	44	50	29	18	36
construction	22	4	0	0	6
trade	10	19	26	25	21
private sector	14	14	24	14	17
public sector	9	13	21	43	21
total (n)	100 (257)	100 (429)	100 (376)	100 (310)	100 (1372)

*Cramer's V : .29, p<.000

Tabular presentation of the figures in the text

Information provided in graphical form in the figures in the text is here presented as tables.

Figure 3.1: Proportion of establishments by share of women in the largest occupational group
Figure 3.2: Gender composition of establishments by sector
Figure 3.3: Gender composition of establishments reporting an increase in part-time and temporary employment contracts
Figure 3.4: Increase in part-time work by country of establishment
Figure 3.5: Sectoral and gender distribution of high qualification work
Figure 3.6: Occupational and gender distribution of high qualification work
Figure 4.1: Gender composition of establishments which practise direct participation
Figure 4.2: Gender composition and different forms of direct participation
Figure 4.3: Gender composition of and form of direct participation used in establishments which have increased part-time work – percentages
Figure 4.4: Gender composition of and form of direct participation used in establishments which have increased temporary work – percentages

Figure 3.1 *Proportion of establishments by share of women in the largest occupational group*

gender composition of establishments	proportion (n)
male-only	23 (1207)
male-dominated	30 (1565)
mixed	25 (1319)
female-dominated	23 (1186)
total	100 (5277)

Appendix

Figure 3.2 *Gender composition of establishments by sector*

	male-dominated (including male-only)	female-dominated
mining	100	0
transport, warehousing and communications	77	5
manufacturing industry	70	11
process industry	67	9
banking/insurance	15	26
professional services	46	23
public utilities	60	23
public administration	32	33
construction and installation	95	3
education	21	36
wholesale	53	16
(public) health and social welfare	16	66
retail trade	23	45
culture and recreation/leisure	11	36
catering, hotels	15	19
average	53	22

Figure 3.3 *Gender composition of establishments reporting an increase in part time and temporary employment contracts*

establishments	male-only	male-dominated	mixed	female-dominated	average of all establishments
reporting an increase in temporary contracts	30	29	27	27	28
reporting an increase in part-time work	6	3	33	41	23

Figure 3.4 *Increase in part-time work by country of establishment*

country	increase in part-time jobs
DK	14
FRA	32
GER	23
IRL	28
ITA	8
NL	29
POR	8
SPA	13
SWE	60
UK	35
average	24

Figure 3.5 *The sectoral and gender distribution of high qualification work*

work requires high qualification in:	male-only	male-dominated	mixed	female-dominated
industry	34	46	16	4
construction	73	21	3	3
trade	10	31	37	22
private services	15	32	40	12
public sector	6	23	33	37

Figure 3.6 *The occupational and gender distribution of high qualification work*

	male-only	male-dominated	mixed	female-dominated
production/transport	38	41	16	5
commercial/personal services	6	32	37	25
medical/education/ administration	3	12	45	40
repair/technical	36	55	7	1

Figure 4.1 *Gender composition of establishments which practise direct participation*

	practises no DP (19%)	practises DP (81%)
male-only	29	21
male-dominated	28	30
mixed	18	27
female-dominated	24	22

Figure 4.2 *Gender composition and different forms of direct participation* (n = 100 per cent)

form of direct participation	male-only (n=914)	male-dominated (n=1291)	mixed (n=1137)	female-dominated (n=944)	average (n=4286)[5]
arm's length individual consultation	45	52	48	43	47
face-to-face individual consultation	36	42	52	45	44
temporary group consultation	39	42	41	36	40
permanent group consultation	33	39	42	38	38
individual delegation	60	66	72	66	66
group delegation	37	40	43	40	40

[5] Minor variations in the total number of cases are possible for every form of DP because of item non-response.

Appendix

Figure 4.3 *Gender composition of and form of direct participation used in establishments which have increased part-time work – percentages*

type of direct participation	male-dominated (including male-only)	mixed	female-dominated
arm's length individual consultation	22	36	51
face-to-face individual consultation	22	40	57
temporary group consultation	24	34	48
permanent group consultation	26	37	56
individual delegation	22	36	47
group delegation	25	40	52

Figure 4.4 *Gender composition of and form of direct participation used in establishments which have increased temporary work – percentages*

type of direct participation	male-dominated (including male-only)	mixed	female-dominated
arm's length individual consultation	60	25	28
face to face individual consultation	68	32	37
temporary group consultation	61	32	29
permanent group consultation	60	22	37
individual delegation	52	28	28
group delegation	61	30	34

European Foundation for the Improvement of Living and Working Conditions

Participating on Equal Terms? The Gender Dimensions of Direct Participation in Organisational Change

Luxembourg: Office for Official Publications of the European Communities

1999 –146 pp. – 16 x 23.5 cm

ISBN 92-828-7146-0

Price (excluding VAT) in Luxembourg: EUR 25